Unlucky Strike

Private Health and the Science, Law and Politics of Smoking

Unlucky Strike

Private Health and the Science, Law and Politics of Smoking

John Staddon

Illustrations and foreword by David Hockney

University of Buckingham Press

First published in Great Britain in 2013 by

The University of Buckingham Press
Yeomanry House
Hunter Street
Buckingham MK18 1EG

A CIP catalogue record for this book is available at the British Library

The front cover photograph is from the author's collection and is what remains of the old American Tobacco cigarette factory in downtown Durham, North Carolina. It is now the signature feature of a cool new smoke-free "American Tobacco Campus" of shops and restaurants.

ISBN 978-1-908684-370

Printed and bound in Great Britain by Marston Book Services Ltd

Dedicated to

Durham, North Carolina
the
Bull City

Table of Contents

Foreword

Life is a killer, we all get only one lifetime and there is only "now". This is my excuse for smoking, but do I really need one if I enjoy it? I have read the cigarette packets (and you can easily get out of the habit of reading them) and all the warnings etc. I accept fate as part of my life and tend to think that to aim for longevity is life denying. I have smoked for sixty years so why stop now.

I know all about the anti-smokers as my father was one; how relentless they are trying to get rid of smoking which they will never do, as there are now more smokers in the world than ever.

Adolf Hitler was the great anti-smoker, and that says it all for me.

David Hockney

Preface

The evils of smoking are a settled issue. Smoking is bad for the smoker and those around him. "Smoking causes lung cancer, bronchitis, emphysema, heart disease and cancers in other organs including the mouth, lip, throat, bladder, kidney, stomach, liver and cervix..." says a prestigious British report[1], feeling no need to document these scary claims. "Half of all smokers will die prematurely" it adds. Environmental tobacco smoke (ETS) is almost as dangerous as mainstream smoke: "ETS has been shown to cause lung cancer and ischaemic heart disease, and probably to cause COPD, asthma and stroke in adults. ETS is harmful to children, causing sudden infant death, pneumonia and bronchitis, asthma, respiratory symptoms and middle ear disease" said the Tobacco Advisory Group of the Royal College of Physicians in July 2005[2]. These conclusions are echoed by every recent official report, from the Surgeon General in the US and to the Royal College of Physicians in the UK and comparable bodies in almost every part of the developed world.

I grew up at a time when almost everyone smoked. I did not see smokers falling from their perches all around me and, as it turns out, most of the smokers I have known have lived to pretty good ages. I had not read these grim reports. When I did, I couldn't help but wonder, just from my own experience, if the dangers of smoking might not be just a wee bit exaggerated.

My personal tipping point occurred when I found out that despite massive publicity to the contrary, smoking has no *public* cost. It puts individual smokers at risk. It does not put the public purse at risk. Strike one against the received view. Prompted by this surprising discovery, I looked further into the facts. The more I looked, the weaker the case against

---

[1] *Public health: ethical issues*. Nuffield Council on Bioethics, 2007. A report prepared by a Working Party chaired by Lord Krebs. p. 105.

[2] *Going smoke-free: The medical case for clean air in the home, at work and in public places*. A report on passive smoking by the Tobacco Advisory Group of the Royal College of Physicians, July 2005. See also *Passive smoking and children*, by the same group, March 2010.

smoking as a *public* health issue became. Is ETS really dangerous to children? How do they know? Does it really cause sudden infant death? How do they know *that*? Proving that smoking can cause an ever-growing list of ailments requires a scientific case that is often impossible to make, for logical, ethical and practical reasons. The case against ETS, in particular, is exceedingly weak.

So, if smoking has no public cost and the medical case for third-party harm is weak, why are smokers victimized in so many ways? I tried to find out – and the answer is not pretty.

Smoking has been controversial ever since tobacco came to Europe in the sixteenth century. Fifty years ago, almost everyone smoked. Fifty years before that, smokers were in the doghouse – cigarettes were illegal in several US states early in the twentieth century. Smoking has always been a ready source of revenue. It has also been a source of health problems, real and imagined. The mixture of pleasure, money and health risk means that smoking is rarely treated fairly by politicians, health professionals or the public. Now, tough anti-smoking laws are almost universal. The misinformation about, and unreasoning hostility directed at, smoking and smokers – and the sight of smokers, usually poor, puffing desperately outside in winter weather – is one reason I wrote this book.

I look at four questions: What *should* we – government, the state – want? “Life, liberty and the pursuit of happiness”? – the US Declaration of Independence implies that the ‘joy of smoking,’ should be part of public policy. Is it? How about health? And longevity? Is a long life for everyone an absolute good? And what about productivity – how much should we value the productive fraction of a citizen’s life? In short, what *is* the common good? Evolutionary biology doesn’t answer these questions, but it should make us skeptical of simple answers to them.

The second question is simply factual: how dangerous is smoking, really? Is it dangerous to others – the problem of secondhand smoke? Well smoking is risky for the smoker, but less risky than most people now believe. It is probably not dangerous to other people.

The third issue is *cost*: Smoking-related illnesses are costly and painful, no doubt. But we all get sick and die; dying is rarely pleasant; and the fact is that smokers tend to die a bit more efficiently than the rest of us. They cost society *less* not more than nonsmokers.

Fourth, what do the answers to these questions tell us about policy? Public cost, possible harm to others, the pleasure smokers get from their habit – and the uncertain value of longevity: how should these guide law and custom? Do actual policies in the US and UK make sense in light of the facts? They do not. The dominant attitude to smoking makes little sense. In addition to an instinctive aversion displayed by a few – an aversion that seems to be more pervasive the rarer smoking becomes – the general animus encourages tendentious science, perverts law and tempts politicians into dubious practices. When large amounts of money can be made at their expense, it's no-win for smokers.

The facts should make society much more relaxed about smoking than it is. But prejudice and perverse incentives in the political and legal systems have pushed policy in the opposite direction. It's time for a re-think and a redress. Let's see if you agree.

John Staddon, Duke University, Durham, North Carolina, July, 2013

The only purpose for which power can be rightfully exercised over any member of a civilized community, against his will, is to prevent harm to others.

(John Stuart Mill)

Many thanks to David Hockney for the pictures

Chapter 1

What is the Common Good?

A Little History

The United States was founded on smoking. The first settlers bet on gold, and lost – but fortunately, John Rolfe arrived soon after with bootlegged Spanish seeds, and the first shipment of Virginia tobacco was sold in London in 1613. Within a year or two the Virginia Company of London began to turn a profit. Tobacco, already popular with the indigenous peoples of the Americas, soon became fashionable: Jamestown's tobacco exports to Europe grew from 10 tons in 1619 to 750 tons in 1639. Saved from extinction by the wonder crop, the new nation was off and running.

But are we grateful? Not really! Even then, not everyone was happy. Tobacco – smoking – is instinctively disliked by some for reasons that are obscure and long predate serious medical research. The revulsion showed itself early in England in the form of a famous 'counterblaste' from King James I (he of the 'King James version' and advocate for the divine right of kings). James, who was also the author of Daemonologie, a tract against witchcraft, in 1604 carried on his campaign against vice by proclaiming that smoking is "A custome lothsome to the eye, hatefull to the Nose, harmefull to the braine, dangerous to the Lungs, and in the blacke stinking fume thereof, neerest resembling the horrible Stigian smoke of the pit that is bottomelesse."[1] Living in a time when disease was thought to be caused by miasmas and the Surgeon General was yet to

---

[1] *A counterblaste to tobacco*. 1604. http://www.gutenberg.org/files/17008/17008-h/17008-h.htm Apparently James' attitude changed when tobacco became a cash crop for Virginia.

report, James lacked science to back him up. But he had no doubt: smoking is bad.

Now tobacco is back in the doghouse again. Such is the current antipathy, I wonder that the politically sensitive do not blame Christopher Columbus more for bringing tobacco to Europe than for bringing Europeans to the Americas. Of course, the Indians are really to blame for discovering the stuff in the first place but, being Indians, they are more easily forgiven (although not by King James, who thought them "pockie," "barbarous," "slavish" and "beastly", among other things!). Tobacco is a gift to historians because of its mysterious power to excite violent antagonism. Memory fades, but in fact smoking was illegal in ten US states in 1909. "In the 1800s, antismoking was a burning issue" writes Cassandra Tate in a fascinating short history[1].

In the mid-twentieth century, scientific evidence was added to visceral dislike and the national war against tobacco was on. The Anglo-American broadcaster Alistair Cooke (1908-2004), a discreet lifelong cigarette smoker himself, summarized the US state of play in 1954 as follows[2]:

> For thirty years or more the scandal sheets have printed articles on "The Tobacco Habit" as a mild variation on their standard high-voltage treatment of such shockers as prostitution, political graft, and the traffic in dope. Most of these pieces, furtively hinting at heart trouble and even tuberculosis, were about as medically convincing as the "Methodist" credo that smoking stunts the growth[3]. The tobacco companies paid only sidelong heed to them, with bold hints that, on the contrary, a cigarette was a relaxant, a soothing syrup, and a social grace. The manufacturers were not much better than the Puritans in their respect for the known scientific facts about tobacco and have tended to meet every impromptu accusation with an equally flip defence. In the social history of our time,

---

[1] Cassandra Tate "In the 1800s, antismoking was a burning issue." *Smithsonian.* 20.n4 (July 1989): 107(9); for even more on smoking's lively history see Jacob Sullum's *For your own good: The anti-smoking crusade and the tyranny of public health.* Free Press, 1998.

[2] Saturday 20 February 1954, http://guardian.co.uk

[3] It does have a small effect on birth weight – see below.

> it may well be that the "Reader's Digest" will come to claim a decisive part in dating the fashion of cigarette smoking.
>
> Although three separate reports were published [in the US] in 1949, suggesting a plausible relationship between smoking and cancer of the lung, they were folded away inside the pages of medical journals. But a year later the "Digest" ran an article with the resounding title "Cancer by the Carton." This started a lot of talk in America and a noticeable adjustment of cigarette advertising to remind the customer that the tobacco companies keep a 24-hour laboratory watch on every chemical intruder that might possibly sully his breath, tickle his throat or otherwise impair his health and comfort. A few of the tobacco companies had in truth been financing quiet research, but it was concerned with heavier matters than a sore throat or an acrid taste. And, since Americans went on buying cigarettes by leaping billions, the manufacturers maintained their code of contemptuous silence…Two years later the "British Medical Journal" published a weightier study and it began to look as if the cigarette manufacturers would never be shut of the nuisance.

True enough. The tobacco companies have never since been 'shut of' this particular nuisance – indeed, many have been since shut down by it. But the victory of the anti-smokers was not immediate. A few eminent statisticians questioned both the numbers and their interpretation. It was not until the latter part of the twentieth century that the health case against smoking was proved.

Economist Paul Krugman writes of Prohibition[1] "It's hard now to appreciate the depth of the fear of alcohol, so extreme that it provoked a constitutional amendment…" Plus ça change…Now, the same hysteria envelops tobacco. As Cassandra Tate puts it: "When US Surgeon General C. Everett Koop declared in May 1988 that cigarettes were as addictive as cocaine and heroin, he was echoing sentiments that had been expressed more than a hundred years earlier." At other times in other places, smokers have been tortured, flogged, excommunicated, had their noses

---

[1] Paul Krugman *The conscience of a liberal: Reclaiming America from the right.* London, Penguin, 2009.

pierced with pipe stems (a kind of homeopathic punishment), exiled to Siberia or murdered in various creative ways. Nowadays we are more civilized – content to let them catch pneumonia as they shiver in winter doorways, shamefacedly dragging on their hyper-taxed coffin nails[1]. These pathetic figures represent the dénouement of the tobacco wars, which took off with James Bonsack's 1880 invention of the cigarette-rolling machine and the entrepreneurial energies of James Buchanan ("Buck") Duke, of blessed memory[2]. Now, more than 130 years later, Duke University, Duke Power Company and the city of Durham, NC, remain. But the boom has ended and it is only a matter of time before the cigar in the hand of Buck Duke's statue on the Duke campus is quietly removed.

The defense of smoking has always been weak. Some physicians in years past saw health or germicidal benefits. Twentieth-century advertisers continued the health theme until forbidden by law[3]. A few clergy saw smoking as a mitigation of alcoholism. Vestiges continue to appear – "natural" cigarettes, for example. On the other hand, nowadays smokers themselves, health-obsessed like everybody else, are embarrassed by or even afraid of their habit, hence raise only feeble resistance to attempts to tax, restrict or penalize it.

So, smoking, an anxious pleasure to smokers, persists. But tobacco continues to scare and annoy. Smoking frightens even more than alcohol whose effects – on the imbiber and on others – can actually be much worse. Fear and distaste continue to foment ill-founded measures that harass smokers in ways that would be regarded as outrageous if the victims were any other group.

---

[1] For amusing accounts of the travails of smokers in New York and California see Happy First Friday of 2012! Victorian Chick and Nina Griscom of *Town and Country* on the Pleasures and Psychology of Smoking.
http://victorianchick.com/2012/01/06/happy-first-friday-of-2012-victorian-chick-and-nina-griscom-of-town-and-country-on-the-pleasures-and-psychology-of-smoking/

[2] Full disclosure: Buck Duke was a founder, with cigarette money, of Duke University, my academic home. For biographical details, see
http://www.anb.org/articles/10/10-00473.html

[3] When no country is mentioned, I am always referring to the US situation.

Health: Public or Private?

Smoking is risky behavior. Smokers tend to die sooner than non-smokers. Smoking is a health problem for smokers, but is it a *public* health problem? Is it bad for the common good? In the US there is no uncertainty. All health issues are treated as public health issues. No distinction is drawn between public and private as far as health is concerned – especially for smoking[1]. Indeed, for smoking there is little distinction between research and advocacy. Even in some of our most distinguished institutions, smoking is treated as worse than a communicable disease. Harvard's School of Public Health is quite proud of its Center for Global Tobacco Control, for example – not Tobacco Research (as in its Center for Biostatistics in AIDS Research) or even Tobacco Analysis (as in the Harvard Center for Risk Analysis). No. Harvard may feel a need to research AIDS and analyze risk, but about tobacco there is no doubt: control is what is required.

Ex-smoker Gregory N. Connolly is head of Harvard's Global Center. He wryly complains about how difficult it is to do anti-smoking research in Massachusetts. Why? Is it because obstacles are raised? Well no, the problem is that there aren't enough smokers! "In Massachusetts, where only 14 percent of people report smoking daily, doing research 'is really, really hard. We just don't have the subjects.'"[2] So how much of a problem is smoking in Massachusetts, really? Not much, it appears. Presumably that's why Dr. Connolly's center has to go global.

I can forgive a health-care professional this kind of one-dimensional view. After all, it's not his business to worry about cost, personal freedom, or even the common good (non-health division). The danger, as I will try

---

[1] The first person I have seen draw the distinction between public and private health (in the case of obesity) is David Boaz in 2004 at http://www.cato.org/pub_display.php?pub_id=2746 More on obesity later.

[2] http://harvardmagazine.com/2011/03/gregory-connolly Harvard is not alone in mixing research with activism. The University of Wisconsin has a Center for Tobacco Research and Intervention, the H. Lee Moffitt Cancer Center & Research Institute has its Tobacco Research and Intervention Program (TRIP), and UCSF has a Center for Tobacco Control Research and Education. Elimination of tobacco use is the unquestioned goal of all academic tobacco research entities.

to show, is that this fixation on the health aspect of every issue has captured government. Smokers have suffered most from this obsession.

The war against smoking has become a secular religion. (Ex-smokers, like most converts, seem to be especially tiresome.) Lacking faith in the sacred, but obsessed with health and retaining vestiges of their Puritan heritage, many Americans have turned to smokers and the obese as the new sinners and objects of righteous wrath.

But there is a difference between public and private health even if it is rarely drawn. After looking at the evidence, I have come to think that quite apart from any supposed 'rights' of smokers, smoking is in fact not bad for the common good. Smoking is a private health problem, not a public health problem. But it isn't treated that way. Questionable science, flawed law, massaged emotion and malign incentives have combined to warp public policy in ways that punish smokers but yield little public gain – even, I will argue, some public loss. This chapter and the next two focus on the science, Chapters 4, 5 and 6 are on law and politics, and Chapter 7 is on ethics.

Longevity, the Individual and the Common Good

So what is the scientific evidence on smoking and how should we interpret it? In developed countries, smokers on average have shorter lives than nonsmokers, so I begin with longevity. Smoking certainly reduces average life expectancy and we all want to live as long as possible, don't we? Well, maybe – or maybe not, if we are enfeebled or in pain. In any case how much should society care about longevity? Then there is the matter of public cost and all the other bad things associated with smoking. But the primary argument against smoking is that it shortens life. That's a reason not to smoke, but is it a reason for society to suppress smoking? That depends on the social value of longevity – an issue that is less simple than it may appear.

The Individual: Health is better than illness. But is illness always better than oblivion, and is life extension always good for everybody? These are harsh questions, but even 300 years ago, before the invention of modern drugs and those ingenious medical systems that serve to prolong indefinitely the lives of the terminally ill and mentally wrecked, people knew that old age is not always a blessing.

Jonathan Swift, in Gulliver's Travels (1726), a satirical science fiction, invented a world of strange creatures – the horse-like, onomatopoeic Houyhnhnms, the tiny Lilliputians, the gigantic Brobdingnagians, and of present interest, the Methuselah-like Struldbruggs. The Struldbruggs were immortal. But they lived not as one might be at the age of thirty, but remained forever at a much more advanced age, eternally troubled by geriatric infirmities. Swift's Gulliver, when he first heard about the Struldbruggs, was filled with envy. But when he got the full story he was less sure: "the Question therefore was not whether a Man would choose to be always in the Prime of Youth, attended with Prosperity and Health, but how he[1] would pass a perpetual Life under all the usual Disadvantages which old Age brings along with it."

Those last years at Sunset Acres are rarely carefree. They are grim for many. As the growing activism for voluntary assisted suicide in various Western countries attests, there is a stage of life when death may seem an improvement. So it was with the Struldbruggs. In Swift's words, "they find themselves cut off from all possibility of Pleasure; and whenever they see a Funeral, they lament and repine that others have gone to a Harbour of Rest, to which they themselves never can hope to arrive." We will all arrive, eventually. But modern medicine ensures that many of us (many more than in the 18th century!) will live to suffer "all the usual disadvantages which old age brings".

Old age was no fun in 1726, but it is in some ways worse now. Life extension is an especially modern problem. I was first struck by this several years ago when I read the marvelous diary of English notable Samuel Pepys, written in cipher in the 1660s (but only decoded and published much later, in 1825). Pepys would occasionally mention that a friend or relative had become sick. But, usually within a week or so, the stricken individual would be either well again – or dead. Protracted infirmity was not the rule in those days as it is nowadays.

---

[1] Swift wrote before the age of political correctness, but I daresay that by "he" and "man" he meant "he or she" and "mankind." In any event, when I use "he" it is generally intended as a generic not a masculine term.

The Group: Longevity is not an absolute good, even for the individual. How about the common good? Well, even if longevity were good for each of us individually, there is reason to doubt it is always good for society – or the species. Long life has aspects of what I have called elsewhere the malign hand, the opposite of Adam Smith's "invisible hand" – good for the individual, maybe, but perhaps not so good for the group[1].

The societal value of longevity is a tough issue because it has to do with the ancient idea of the good, something that has puzzled philosophers from Aristotle to G. E. Moore. Some things are good in and of themselves – nourishment, clean water, kindness, health, life, liberty and the pursuit of most kinds of happiness. These things we can call absolute goods and they are the sort of things written into ethical codes like the ten commandments. But other things are good because of their effects – these are instrumental or utilitarian goods: means, not ends in themselves. Penicillium mould is good because it helps cure disease, but there is nothing intrinsically good about fungus. Calcium chloride is useful for de-icing roads in winter, but is not itself considered to be a holy substance.

We tend to think of longevity as falling in the former class rather than the latter, an absolute good, not good because of its effects. But Swift depicted old age as a burden for many and modern medicine has if anything increased the possibilities for extended suffering. I remember my own grandmother, crippled and in pain from cancer in her late eighties, wishing for release[2]. Extreme old age was not good for her and medicine had little to offer but prolonging her distress.

I will show next that in terms of another good, the persistence (sustainability) – of the species or of a culture – longevity of the individual has mixed effects. Population biology shows that average lifespan in any species is highly sensitive to the rigors of natural selection.

---

[1] John Staddon: *The Malign Hand of the Markets: The Insidious Forces on Wall Street that are Destroying Financial Markets—and What We Can Do About it* McGraw-Hill, 2012.

[2] A chilling description of the emotional and financial problems of caring for the aged is Sandra Loh's article: Daddy Issues: Why caring for my aging father has me wishing he would die (*The Atlantic* March 2012) which describes Loh's own family and reviews three books on the topic.

For some organisms, under some conditions, a long lifespan is good, for others under other conditions, it is bad.

There is a whole area of biological research devoted to so-called life-history strategies[1], the ways that selective forces affect the duration of, and physical changes during, typical lifespan. Lifespan depends on the environment, the organism's niche in eco-jargon; that is, on the selection pressures under which the species evolved. It turns out that a longer life is not always better from the point of view of evolutionary success.

Lifespan is strongly subject to natural selection. Experiments, both natural and in the laboratory, have shown the effects of environment on inherited lifespan. For example, in one early experiment[2], fruit flies – *Drosophila*, the lab rat of experimental genetics – were selected for late breeding. That is to say, breeders for the next generation were taken from the longest-lived flies; short-lived flies had no offspring. Lifespan correspondingly increased from generation to generation as Darwin would have predicted. The response to selection for early breeding was more variable. The main point is that typical lifespan depends on Darwinian fitness. If late breeders have more offspring, organisms will mature later and live longer.

In nature, different species have different lifespans and it's pretty obvious that variants that develop and breed quickly will often be 'fitter' – have more offspring per year, and greater population growth – than those who live longer but breed later. Which strategy works better depends on the environment. A well-known study looked at opossums in Georgia, either on the mainland, where some 50% of natural deaths were caused by predators, or on Sapelo Island, where none were, because the island has no large mammals.[3] Mainland possums bred earlier than Sapelo possums, as evolutionary theory would predict. They adapted to the threat of predation by reproducing as quickly as possible.

Environmental effects are sometimes surprising. For example, guppies are small, ovoviviparous tropical fish popular for home aquariums. In

---

[1] http://en.wikipedia.org/wiki/Life_history_theory

[2] Luckinbill, L. S., & Clare, M. J. (1985) Selection for life span in *Drosophila melanogaster*. *Heredity*, 55, 9-18.

[3] Austad, S. N. (1993) Retarded senescence in an insular population of Virginia opossums (*Didelphus virginiana*). *Journal of Zoology, London,* 229:695-708.

nature they live in a variety of freshwater environments, some with large predators, some with small or no predators. Researchers in California recently found that guppies living in environments with a large number of predators reproduce earlier in life than guppies that have low predation levels. However, if they survive predation, the guppies from high-predation localities live far longer, on average, than guppies from low-predation localities, indicating that high-predation guppies inherit a longer "reproductive period" – the time between first and last reproduction.[1] Guppies from high-predation environments live – and reproduce for – longer. The pain of predation is evidently counterbalanced to some degree by a longer reproductive period.

The adaptive details differ from species to species, but the evolutionary bottom line is always reproduction, Darwinian fitness. Under many conditions, fast breeding, short-lived variants may out-compete long-lived, but slower-breeding types.

What is abundantly clear is that in nature a long life is not an absolute good. Sometimes a short and happy (= reproductive) life is way better for evolutionary success than a long and less fecund one. Lifespan is nature's planned obsolescence.

Longevity and Human Evolution: Extending this kind of thinking to human society is of course risky. Most people just assume that a society of long-lived people is better (certainly) and more successful (probably) than one whose citizens die earlier. But is that always true? After all, it isn't easy to figure out why some cultural groups persist while others vanish. The forces that cause one group, like the Shakers, to exit the scene while others, such as Moslems or Mormons, grow and persist, are usually hard to identify with certainty. In fact, the reason the Shakers died out is more obvious than most: they believed in celibacy, hence could renew themselves only through conversion – a task not made easier by the belief that made it necessary. But reproductive patterns can change from one generation to the next and other factors can intervene. Predictions can never be certain. Nevertheless, the effect of cultural norms on what might be called 'cultural fitness' should surely play some part in our judgments of what is good and bad for society.

---

[1] Fish evolve a longer lifespan by evolving a longer period during which they reproduce, researchers find. http://newsroom.ucr.edu/cgi-bin/display.cgi?id=1209

Our beliefs – opposition to or tolerance for abortion, equal status for women, democracy, free speech, avoidance of risk, belief in the value of longevity itself – are part of our culture. But if any belief is detrimental to the survival of that culture – like the celibacy of the Shakers – its value may be questioned. Few would defend a belief that is certain to lead to cultural extinction[1]. The usual assumption is that anything that helps us to live longer is good and conversely, anything that shortens life is bad. But that assumption rests on another: that longer lifespan is always better for the common good.

But is it? What role does longevity play in the success of a culture? Evolutionary biology suggests that there is an optimal lifespan that differs from species to species. The optimal lifespan is never infinite. Are humans exempt from these limitations? Almost certainly not.

In evolutionary biology, the idea of group selection was for many years dismissed, mainly because selection acting on individuals – which favors selfish behavior – will always (it was thought) act faster than selection for altruism, which favors one group over another. Recently, however, increasingly plausible scenarios have been proposed in which the genes for group-favoring altruism[2] may increase even in populations of non-human animals. So, even at the genetic level, group-benefiting behavior may be selected for.

Competition and conflict between nations is a constant in human history. "War is not the answer!" "The meek shall inherit the earth!" Nice ideas, but unfortunately very often it is and they don't. History has grayed-out the records of countless groups that were beaten in war and extinguished, either literally or by assimilation by their conquerors. Either

---

[1] For a fuller discussion of this complex issue see Staddon, J. E. R.(2004) Scientific imperialism and behaviorist epistemology. *Behavior and Philosophy, 32*, 231-242. http://dukespace.lib.duke.edu/dspace/handle/10161/3389_and Staddon J. Faith, fact and behaviorism. *The Behavior Analyst,* 2013, in press.

[2] There are no literal "genes for altruism" of course. But this expression is less cumbersome than (say) "the heritable basis for altruistic behavior." On the current status of group selection, see, for example, http://web.missouri.edu/~ernstz/phil_bio/reintroducing.pdf and http://www.iep.utm.edu/altr-grp/ for reviews. An excellent popular account of a major controversy surrounding the biology of altruism is by Jonah Lehrer: Dept. of Science, "Kin and Kind," *The New Yorker*, March 5, 2012, p. 36 http://archives.newyorker.com/?i=2012-03-05#folio=036

way, their core cultural beliefs were lost. War, in its various forms, often works. And violent death was much more common in the past, when human beings were molded by natural selection, than it has been in the recent century, a time too short for much evolutionary change.[1] War has played a huge role in the development of the human race.

Success in war requires altruism by warriors: courage, daring and a willingness to die – characteristics dangerous to oneself but, during wartime, beneficial to the group. Altruism favors the group over the individual and often the altruist will have a shorter life than his conspecifics. In other words, a short lifespan is not necessarily bad for the species.

The social processes favoring altruism in humans are obvious. Warfighters, willing to give their lives for their country, are universally lauded. A few striking exceptions (such as Winston Churchill and Douglas MacArthur, both of whom ran extraordinary risks as young soldiers) notwithstanding, a courageous and daring warrior is not apt to live long. Yet such warriors have many times proved necessary to the survival of their cultures. A universal practice, as Darwin noted, is to reward the families of fallen warriors – a direct genetic-fitness benefit[2] to the slain warrior and a counterbalance to the loss of (evolutionary) fitness associated with his death. In accordance with this tradition, when he was in a position to do so Iraq's Saddam Hussein offered to donate $25,000 to the family of each successful Palestinian suicide bomber.

Suicide bombing itself is deplored by groups that are its victims, but perhaps more for its typical targets, innocent civilians, than for the practice itself. Japan's kamikaze pilots, whose targets were military (Allied naval ships), were respected, to a degree, by their adversaries. Civilian-targeting jihadi 'martyrs' and Tamil Tigers are not.

---

[1] A surprising conclusion, well documented by Steven Pinker in *The Better Angels Of Our Nature: Why Violence Has Declined*. Viking (2011). See also almost any of Winston Churchill's writings about the colonial period, or Niall Ferguson's *Civilization: The West and the Rest* (Penguin, 2012), for vivid descriptions of our violent past.

[2] Because his relatives, who share his genes, are favored. This is an *inclusive fitness* argument, made famous in a paper by W. Hamilton in 1964. (http://en.wikipedia.org/wiki/Inclusive_fitness). The idea has come in for some criticism recently, but selection pressures on relatives are clearly an important component of Darwinian fitness.

Whether you approve of suicide bombers or not, most would agree that longevity, at least in the context of war, cannot be an overriding value. In war, personal survival is not the highest good. And success in war has undoubtedly played a role in the persistence of cultures.

Even in peacetime, the race is not always to the long-lived. Israel and its Islamic foes provide a vivid example. In 1947, a year before the partition of India, the UN recommended partition of Palestine, then also under the control of the British, and the re-creation of a Jewish state. Conflict between Jews and Arabs intensified. Many in Britain favored the creation of Israel, but pro-Arab forces delayed the decision until Zionist militants forced the issue. In 1948 the British left and, shortly after, the first of several Arab-Israeli wars began.

This continuing conflict is a highly asymmetrical one. Jewish Israel is a first-world country with a developed technological economy (more NASDAQ listings than the entire Arab world, for example[1]), modern agriculture and considerable wealth. Moslem-Arab Palestine, on the other hand, is much poorer and less self-sufficient. As two major wars attest, in any straightforward military conflict there is little doubt who would win.

Israelis are also very healthy. The life expectancy of Jewish Israeli men is among the highest of all developed countries, just one year below Japan, which is number one. The average life expectancy in Israel in 2005 was 82.4 years for women and 78.3 years for men. The figures for the Moslem Arab population of Israel are somewhat lower and getting worse: The life expectancy of an Arab male in 2005 was 3.1 years shorter than that of a Jewish male, as opposed to a two-year difference in 1999. The difference between the life expectancies for Jewish and Arab females in Israel has risen from 3.1 years to 3.6 years since 1999.

On the other hand, the rate of annual population growth of the Jewish population stood at 1.5 percent in 2005, while the rate of growth of the Muslim population was 3 percent[2]. Thus the shorter-lived Moslem population is growing at twice the rate of the longer-lived Jewish population. This is a huge difference. Should it persist, and if all else remains the same, there is no doubt that the Arab-Muslim population will soon become the majority, despite its shorter average lifespan. Of course,

[1] *USA Today,* May 23, 2011.

[2] http://www.haaretz.com/hasen/spages/764944.html

all else is not necessarily going to remain the same. Religious conversion, accommodation, cultural assimilation, inter-marriage, migration and further wars – many purely cultural processes may counterbalance or even reverse reproduction-rate effects.

Nevertheless, the same process may now be operating in many other places. There is alarm in European countries like The Netherlands and even Belgium and Norway, that fecund and cohesive immigrant populations, usually Moslem but sometimes from other cultures, will swamp the indigenous culture. In 2009, the name 'Mohammed' became the majority choice for male babies in the four largest Dutch cities[1]. In 2010 Mohammed became the most popular name for newborn boys in Britain[2]. Serious discussion of these facts is often dismissed as alarmist if not racist. But you don't need to take sides to count – or to see that longevity per se doesn't necessarily conduce to the survival of a culture.

Longevity and Sickness: Even a high incidence of fatal illness may have surprisingly little effect on measures of national success such as prosperity. Botswana, for example, currently has the highest incidence of HIV-AIDS in sub-Saharan Africa (26.5%)[3] and one of the shorter life expectancies (49.8 years in 2006 vs. 50.7 for South Africa and 53.9 for Kenya) but it's also the richest African country, with a slightly higher gross national income per capita than South Africa ($5680 vs. $5390) and much higher than Kenya ($580). Longevity is only one of many factors that affect the success of a culture, however that may be measured.

These surprising facts show that measures to reduce disease have mixed effects on an economy. Cure for a chronic and debilitating, if not fatal, condition is likely to be a great benefit. Curing a fast-acting killer disease, especially one that preferentially affects the old, may have zero economic benefit or even a collective cost.

Good data on the comparative effects of curing different types of disease are rare. One example is reported in an article headlined "Improved health does not always make countries richer" in *The*

---

[1] London *Daily Telegraph*, August 14, 2009.

[2] http://www.dailymail.co.uk/news/article-1324194/Mohammed-popular-baby-boys-ahead-Jack-Harry.html

[3] http://www.avert.org/subaadults.htm; http://web.worldbank.org/WBSITE/

Economist magazine.[1] It describes an intervention in Colombia: "Studying the impact of the eradication of malaria in Colombia, [the researcher] noted that parts of the country were affected by a species of the malarial parasite called *Plasmodium vivax*, which led to very poor health but was rarely fatal. The more lethal version, *P. falciparum*, affected other areas. He found that eliminating *P. vivax* led to significant gains in human capital and income; eliminating *P. falciparum* did not." In other words, it is better for the country as a whole that sick people die quickly rather than lingering on in impaired state. Better to cure the lingering illness than the truly lethal one.

The Economist, reluctant to make the obvious inference, concluded "It may be best to make a case for improving health [longevity] because it is a good thing in itself, rather than on the basis of presumed economic benefits that may not appear for generations." The fact is that longevity may be good or bad – for the individual and for the community. It all depends on the details.

How does smoking fit in? Is it a slow, debilitating disease or a fast-acting killer? As we'll see, smoking is closer to the latter than the former. It affects its victims rather late in life and they spend if anything a shorter time in a debilitated condition than nonsmokers. So are countries with lots of smokers richer than countries with a smaller percentage? This is an impossible question to answer, given all the other differences between countries. I have looked at the correlation[2] between smoking incidence (% of smokers in the population) and either life expectancy or GDP/capita, for 17 countries, from Switzerland to Sri Lanka and found zero correlation for life expectancy and a small negative correlation for wealth: wealthier countries smoke a bit less. Whether smoking suppresses wealth or vice versa is of course unknown. The small size of the correlation and the many uncontrolled differences among countries make this kind of exercise of questionable value in any case. But, as we will see, reservations like

---

[1] *The Economist*. London: Nov 22, 2008. Vol. 389, Iss. 8607

[2] Based on data from Appendix IV of: *International Smoking Statistics*. A collection of historical data from 30 economically developed countries, 2nd edition, Barbara Forey, Jan Hamling, Peter Lee, Nicholas Wald, editors. Wolfson Institute of Preventive Medicine and Oxford University Press, London and Oxford; 2002.

this rarely deter health-promoting agencies from affirming the evils of smoking when correlations come out in the preferred direction.

The data show that smoking shortens life with a relatively small probability and by a relatively small average amount in a way exacts no collective cost. Should not the decision on whether to smoke or not therefore be up to the individual? Unless, like the hapless Struldbruggs, we wish to include longevity in our pantheon of absolutes – like truth, justice, happiness, liberty and maybe a few others – measures to enhance longevity need to be weighed against other values and other costs and benefits. This most emphatically we do not do. The next chapter looks at science and smoking in more detail.

A GLASS
ASHTRAY
in case you
had forgotten

Chapter 2

Smoking Science, non-Science and Nonsense

Cigarette smoking and, to a lesser extent other forms of tobacco use, is generally regarded as a major public-health problem. Smoking is certainly risky for the smoker, but whether it imposes the kind of collective cost that would make it a public health problem is much less clear. Five charges are leveled against smoking and smokers:

1. Smoking is unpleasant, certainly unpopular, and probably immoral (cigarette taxes are usually lumped with taxes on alcohol as *sin* taxes).
2. Smoking is lethal to smokers.
3. Smoking is addictive.
4. Smoking injures non-smokers (the problem of secondhand smoke).
5. Smoking is costly to society: it is a public health problem.

How valid are these claims, and what should governments do about smoking? In fact after decades of controversy, there is now little public dispute. Too little, as we'll see.

Evil: First, smoking is deemed morally bad. Smokers have no right to smoke outside their own homes – and perhaps not even inside if they have kids or live in close proximity to others. Smoking in public spaces, bars and restaurants included, is verboten through most of the EU and much of the US. Bans have been adopted even by one-time tobacco states. In Durham, North Carolina, a city founded on tobacco, a sign outside a newly enlarged branch public library warns patrons that smoking is "forbidden within 50 feet" of the building.

Yet, personal health risks apart, if smoking is a sin it is a pretty benign one. (What about secondhand smoke and harm to others, I hear you cry!

We'll get to that in the next chapter.) Many very successful people, good and evil, from Winston Churchill to Joseph Stalin – and most of The Greatest Generation[1] – were smokers. Unlike alcohol, tobacco doesn't impair mental activity or cause smokers to act stupid or violent. Despite the taboos, there is as yet no DWS – "driving-while-smoking" – charge in any state. Indeed, many really smart, productive (even long-lived!) people have been smokers. Many smokers believe that smoking actually helps them concentrate and there is some supporting evidence[2]. If more proof is needed, just remember that Sherlock Holmes always referred to a difficult case as "a three-pipe problem"! In dreary faux-ironic surrender to modern taboos, Benedict Cumberbatch, who plays Holmes in a recent BBC series, instead of Sherlock's calabash, is forced to resort to nicotine patches. (Somehow "three-patch problem" doesn't have quite the same resonance!)

Here is an unscientific sample of famous smokers, good and bad: Winston Churchill, Franklin Delano Roosevelt, Joseph Stalin, Ayn Rand, Deng Xiaoping (Chinese leader) Albert Einstein, Konrad Lorenz (Nobel-winning German biologist), Sigmund Freud, Werner Heisenberg (Nobel-winning German physicist), Claude Monet (French impressionist painter), Pablo Picasso, Bertrand Russell (English mathematician and philosopher). Only two – Freud and Monet – died of a smoking-related diseases (at 83 and 86, respectively[3]). The others lived to ages ranging from 63 (FDR) to 98 (Russell). The list of eminent alcoholics and creative drug users is much shorter – a few musicians and writers might qualify, but the list of successful mathematicians, scientists and philosophers with these habits is short to zero.

Lethal: How about lethality? "*They know they're killing themselves*" said űber-rich ex-smoker and anti-smoking zealot New York City Mayor Michael Bloomberg. Is smoking really *lethal* as Hizzoner avers? No. Mayor Bloomberg should check out his own news service, which reported in March 2011 on the death of Mississippi-born blues pianist Pinetop

[1] http://en.wikipedia.org/wiki/Greatest_Generation

[2] For example, http://www.webmd.com/smoking-cessation/news/20021023/harnessing-nicotines-power

[3] Ayn Rand was operated on for lung cancer in 1974 but died of heart failure eight years later. Smoking-related death? Possibly.

Perkins: "...who started a solo career in his 70s after performing with fellow bluesman Muddy Waters for more than a decade... Perkins [who died at 97] outlived most of his peers even though he smoked from the age of 9, battled alcoholism into his 80s and ate at McDonald's Corp.'s fast-food restaurants daily." Like three quarters of his fellow smokers, Perkins died of something other than a smoking-related disease.

Cigarette smoking is certainly risky, but identifying smoking as a cause – of death or disease – is in fact much more difficult than people think. Human experiments cannot be done and the effects of smoking are delayed for many years. If a smoker dies of lung cancer, you can be pretty sure smoking was the cause because it is a rare disease and relatively few non-smokers get it. The *risk ratio* (also called the odds ratio), smokers/nonsmokers, in the US is about 8 to 1 (larger for heavy smokers; three to one in a recent Chinese study)[1]. That is to say, a smoker has eight times the chance of dying of lung cancer than a matched (aye, there's the rub!) non-smoker. But heart attacks cause the deaths of many non-smokers as well as smokers. The relative-risk ratio is usually only two or less, which is normally thought to be too small to be reliable given all the possible confounding variables (i.e., unmeasured differences between smoker and non-smokers other than their smoking habits). For a common cause of death like heart attack, identifying smoking as the cause of any particular death – or even as a risk factor – is essentially impossible. Although life expectancy is the best measure of the bad effects of smoking, it's also far from perfect because smokers and non-smokers differ in many ways other than their smoking habits.[2]

Proving that a given death is smoking-related is in fact very difficult, as we will see. Nevertheless, since 1965 government-mandated warnings on cigarette packets express no doubts. "Smoking Kills" is the most common, "Smoking May Cause Impotence" the most ridiculous given the proven fecundity of generations of smokers. The Greatest Generation, smokers mostly, was a great deal more progenitive than the generations

---

[1] http://www.ncbi.nlm.nih.gov/pubmed/20193225

[2] See, for example Smoking and risk of myocardial infarction in women and men: longitudinal population study. Prescott E; Hippe M; Schnohr P; Hein HO; Vestbo J, *BMJ* 1998 Apr 4;316(7137):1043-7.

that came after, who smoked less, for example. And in any case, as everyone knows, you smoke *afterwards*!

Ridiculous or not, the warnings seem to work. Along with steady increases in tobacco taxes and other imposts, negative advertising seems to have caused cigarette sales to decline in most recent years. Cigarette companies certainly know that people are afraid of their products. In 2010 the Chinese started offering in the US a "safe" electronic cigarette, presented in advertisements by a heavily made-up young woman, lips invitingly parted behind a wreath of (fake) smoke. E-cigarettes now promise to become a major industry[1]. US manufacturers offered "light" and mentholated cigarettes for many years, playing up the health aspect. Most cigarettes sold now are filter-tipped. Recently, "natural" cigarettes (whatever they may be) have been advertised in upscale magazines. People are scared and manufacturers know it. But how dangerous are cigarettes, really?

Cigarette smoking is not in fact *lethal* like, say, falling from a tall building, taking an overdose of cyanide or playing Russian roulette with one in the chamber. But it is *risky*, like riding a motorcycle (with or without a helmet), bungee-jumping, hang-gliding, riding horses or luges – or indiscriminate sex.

How risky is it? People actually exaggerate the risk as Harvard law and economics professor Kip Viscusi pointed out in a 2002 article on tobacco regulation: "...do people realize the extent of life that might be lost because of smoking? Scientific estimates of that loss are in the range of six to eight years. However, the public's risk perception is greater, as men believe the life expectancy loss is 10.1 years and women believe that it is 14.8 years."[2] The worst you can say is that "smoking is by far the largest single risk that most people take."

---

[1] http://www.nytimes.com/2013/06/13/business/e-cigarettes-are-in-vogue-and-at-a-crossroads.html?_r=0

[2] The New Cigarette Paternalism, By W. Kip Viscusi, REGULATION, Winter 2002 – 2003. A comprehensive survey, *The Price of Smoking, by* Frank A. Sloan, Jan Ostermann, Christopher Conover, Donald H. Taylor, Jr. and Gabriel Picone (MIT Press, 2004) summarizes the data up to 2002.

In fact, between one and 32% of smoker deaths across the world are smoking-related[1]. The percentage is smaller in developing than developed countries, because you have to *not* die from other causes to live long enough to die from smoking-related disease.[2] In the third world, the bad effects of smoking are pre-empted by malnutrition, accidents and infectious disease. Might as well smoke, if you're gonna die anyway! Between 20 and 30% of US smokers die of smoking-related diseases. Not good, of course, but much less than the "100% lethal" implied by packet warnings and Mayor Bloomberg. And we all die eventually, so the real issue is not death *per se*, but the time and manner of death.

There are reasons to believe that the real proportion of smoking-caused deaths in the US may be lower than the numbers suggest. First, the data are always *associations* not identified *causes*. The figures show the number of people in categories – died but didn't smoke, vs. died and smoked (how much? for how long?). They are just correlations, which matters because the source of a correlation is always uncertain. A and B may be associated because both are caused by some third thing, C – or B may cause A rather than the reverse. Thus we need to be sure that smokers are in other respects *exactly the same* as the population of non-smokers with which they are being compared. Otherwise we can't be sure that the higher death rate of smokers is not because they are less healthy or more susceptible for some other reason.

Are smokers and non-smokers identical in every other respect? Well, no they're not – and the differences are probably growing. A few decades ago almost everybody smoked: upper, lower and middle class. Check out those 1950s movies, TV through the mid-1990s, the recent 1960s TV drama *Mad Men,* or videos of NASA's space-shuttle mission control as

---

[1] A comprehensive correlational study of cigarette mortality is: Mortality in relation to smoking: 50 years' observations on male British doctors. By Richard Doll, Richard Peto, Jillian Boreham, Isabelle Sutherland. *BMJ*, doi:10.1136/bmj.38142.554479.AE (published 22 June 2004). The authors conclude that lifelong smokers lose about 10 years of life. But again, although the subject population was all male doctors, the smoking and non-smoking sub-populations are not identical: the smokers apparently drank almost more than twice as much alcohol per week as the nonsmokers, for example.

[2] Ezzati M, Lopez AD. Estimates of global mortality attributable to smoking in 2000. *Lancet*, 2003; 362(9387):847-852.

late as the 1980s! Many people are smoking in these images. Free cigarettes were issued as morale-boosters in the US army and handed out to visitors to cigarette factories. But in recent years, as smoking has been effectively stigmatized, increasingly it is the poor who tend to smoke, and the middle and upper classes, better nourished, less obese – healthier – who do not. So perhaps something else, some other variable, accounts for (all? some?) of the difference in mortality rates between smokers and non-smokers?

Or the association between smoking and a shorter lifespan may be accidental – after all, if we accept the (absurdly-relaxed-but-conventional) five percent level of statistical significance, at least one in twenty correlations *will* be spurious[1]. Most negative results – failures to find any difference between smokers and non-smokers – will not be published at all[2]. Consequently, the balance of evidence is likely to be much less clear than what is claimed.

Problems like this were enough to raise questions in the mind of Sir Ronald Aylmer Fisher (1890-1962), the father of modern statistics. Fisher was clever even as a boy. He went to Harrow, the famous British 'public' school, also host to Jawaharlal Nehru and, some years earlier, to Winston Churchill. Asked to name the dozen or so most brilliant boys of his acquaintance, a master at the school responded "it would be difficult to do so but added that on sheer brilliance he could divide all those he had taught into two groups: one contained a single outstanding boy, R. A. Fisher, the other all the rest."[3] Fisher lived up to his promise by going on

---

[1] Many more than one in twenty in most cases, in fact. The standard null-hypothesis-testing statistical methodology has come under increasing attack recently. See, for example, *Perspectives in Psychological Science*, 7(6) 528–530, 2012, Editors' Introduction to the Special Section on Replicability in Psychological Science: A Crisis of Confidence? Harold Pashler and Eric–Jan Wagenmakers. For more discussion see J. Staddon, *The New Behaviorism,* Chapter 9, in press.

[2] See, for example "Publication Probity", http://www.nytimes.com/2006/12/10/magazine/10section3a.t-4.html and *Wall Street Journal,* article (12/02/11) "Scientists' Elusive Goal: Reproducing Study Results" by Gautam Naik. See also John Staddon, *The New Behaviorism,* in press, Chapter 9; B. A. Williams (2010), Perils of evidence-based medicine. *Perspectives in Biology and Medicine*, 53(1), 106–20.

[3] R. A. Fisher: An Appreciation. E. B. Ford. *Genetics* 171: 415–417 (October 2005)

to invent much of modern statistics. But in 1958 he disputed the conclusion of fellow UK researchers Dr. Bradford Hill and Sir Richard Doll that cigarettes are a cause of lung cancer[1].

Apropos correlation and causation, Fisher wrote: "I remember Professor Udny Yule in England pointing to one which illustrates my purpose sufficiently well. He said that in the years in which a large number of apples were imported into Great Britain, there were also a large number of divorces. The correlation was large, statistically significant at a high level of significance, unmistakable. But no one, fortunately, drew the conclusion that the apples caused the divorces or that the divorces caused the apples to be imported." After reviewing the evidence on smoking and cancer, Fisher concluded: "For my part, I think it is more likely that a common cause supplies the explanation." meaning that his best guess was that smoking and lung cancer were both caused by some third thing – inflammation, a pre-cancerous condition, whatever – rather than one being the cause of the other.

This is not what we believe now, of course, but it is a good illustration of *the limitations of epidemiology*. I haven't counted them all, but my impression is that at least 80-90% of the health-related 'studies' reported in the media are epidemiological. They are just correlations – between divorce and apple imports or between disease and some other characteristic. (One that for some reason sticks in my mind is "Salad Dressing Link to Prostate Cancer Survival"[2].) Epidemiology is a useful source of hypotheses. It should never be taken as conclusive evidence of cause. Yet almost invariably, associations, especially if they fit people's preconceptions, are reported as causes.

If the link is plausible, and the issue one that arouses general fear, these 'studies' can do enormous harm. The most infamous recent example of correlation falsely interpreted as causation is an apparent link between the MMR (measles-mumps-rubella) vaccine and the very distressing condition of autism, which tends to appear in the first three years of life. The supposed MMR-autism link first appeared in a 1998 study with a

---

[1] Fisher, R. A. (1958) Cigarettes, cancer and statistics. *The Centennial Review* v.2: 151-166. http://digital.library.adelaide.edu.au/coll/special/fisher/274.pdf

[2] How exactly is the dressing to be administered, one wonders? London *Daily Telegraph,* June 11, 2013.

handful of patients by one Dr. Andrew Wakefield in England. Wakefield's study was later shown to be flawed if not faked but the large number of MMR injections then typically given to each child and the presence of mercury (mercury!) in vaccine preservative made Wakefield's hypothesis very believable to countless anxious parents of autistic children[1]. The celebrity and onetime Playboy bunny Jenny McCarthy, for example, whose child appeared for a time to be autistic, embarked on a crusade to block vaccination. No doubt many thousands of children and adults (for whom it can be fatal) caught measles and the other diseases on account of the vaccines they did *not* receive, as a consequence of public alarm raised by Wakefield's study. A measles outbreak in Wales in 2013 has been traced to parents' reluctance to vaccinate, in response to Wakefield's spurious study.

Similar, if less dramatic, scenarios are played out as a result of a steady stream of studies linking obesity, meat, sugar, salt, TV watching, video games or whatever to various societal ills. Correlations all – but they often prompt action in the gullible even though causation is never proved.

There usually isn't a problem if the observed correlation is obviously meaningless, as in the apples-divorces case. But when it is plausible, like a link between smoking – first-, second- or even third-hand – and various heart and lung ailments, many perhaps most people, like Mayor Bloomberg, will leap immediately from correlation to causation and assume that smoking, of whatever degree, is the cause of the ailment. Indeed, it may be. But, absent an essential step, *experiment, we do not know.*

An example where correlation did turn out to be causation is the famous case of Dr. John Snow who, in the 1850s tried to figure out the causes of cholera epidemics in London[2]. He began by noticing the significantly higher incidence of the disease in an area in Soho served by a particular water pump – a classic epidemiological finding. The germ theory of disease was yet to be discovered, but Snow nevertheless guessed that contaminated water might be the cause. But the key to solving the

[1] See, for example, Sharon Begley, "Anatomy of a scare" NEWSWEEK, Feb 21, 2009, from the magazine issue dated Mar 2, 2009.

[2] http://en.wikipedia.org/wiki/John_Snow_%28physician%29

problem was not the correlation between cholera incidence and a particular location. The correlation merely suggested the hypothesis. The clincher was Snow's experimental test. When he disabled the water pump, cholera incidence dropped dramatically. Experiment, or deep understanding of the underlying disease process, is essential to proving causation. Not only is correlation alone insufficient, by itself a correlation can be downright misleading.

'Third variables' – the possibility that smokers and non-smokers differ in ways that might account for mortality differences – can be allowed for ('controlled') statistically in various ways and the techniques for doing so continue to evolve[1]. But the controls depend on assumptions (additivity, independence, knowing the relevant variables, etc.) that may not be true – and whose truth cannot easily be assessed. We'll see in a moment that the additivity assumption is violated by at least one smoking-and-health data point. Statistical 'controls' are no substitute for controlled experiment. In the absence of experiment or full understanding of the causal processes involved, *any* correlation is suspect.

Of course (again in Fisher's words) "It is not the fault of Hill or Doll or Hammond that they cannot produce [experimental] evidence in which a thousand children of teen age have been laid under a ban that they shall never smoke, and a thousand more chosen at random from the same age group have been under compulsion to smoke at least thirty cigarettes a day. If that type of experiment could be done, there would be no difficulty [in proving a causal relationship between smoking and disease]." Now, of course, the evidence is overwhelming that cigarette smoking is bad for you, but just *how* bad, and for whom, is much less clear.

Addictive: Is smoking addictive? Depends what you mean by *addictive*, of course, but yes, by most definitions it is, though not for everyone. Even as long ago as the 1930s the addictive properties of cigarettes were well-enough known that the Third Reich had an ad campaign against them. A typical ad, translated, ran: "He does not devour it [the cigarette], it devours him! Signed: The Chainsmoker". Adolf Hitler, a vegetarian and dog lover, was also a passionate anti-smoker.[2] His

---

[1] See Sloan et al., *op. cit.* for the state of statistics as of 2004.

[2] *The Nazi War on Cancer,* by Robert N. Proctor (Princeton U. P. 1991). See also http://en.wikipedia.org/wiki/Anti-tobacco_movement_in_Nazi_Germany

government propagandized that smoking cost the state the equivalent of 2 million Volkswagens a year, a claim about as accurate as most National Socialist claims, as we'll see in a moment.

Infamously, in 1994 seven US tobacco-company executives testified before ex-smoker Henry Waxman's congressional committee that nicotine (five of them) or nicotine and tobacco products (two) are not addictive. Were they mendacious, ill-advised – or partly correct? Perhaps all of the above. The problem is that although addiction sounds like a scientific term, it is not. To say that someone is addicted is much more problematic than saying he has an infection or a fever. Addiction is not a well-defined medical term like inflammation. 'Addiction' has no physiological signature. There is no reason to doubt that the physiological mechanisms are the same for the 'addicted' person as for the non-addicted: "As honest experts will admit, there is no consensual definition of 'addiction' within any of the specialty disciplines that study the condition, and there is no definitive biological marker for it."[1]

'Addiction' has moral overtones. We don't accuse doting mothers of being addicted to their children or hungry workers of being addicted to their food – unless the child is judged to be spoiled or the workers seen to be fat. Whatever medical or physiological differences may exist between addict and non-addict, they are unlikely to be simple enough to be described by a single term.

Most addicts are also conflicted about their habit: they want to give it up, but can't. Tobacco is addictive in this sense; many fearful smokers want to give up smoking but find themselves unable to do so. Two thirds of US smokers say they want to quit, a third try each year but only about 3% succeed[2]. Clearly many are not serious about quitting. In a group of 11,791 smokers, 41% said they would like to attend a free stop-smoking clinic, but when one was actually set up, only 3% actually turned up.[3] But for many people, eating is also addictive in this sense, as the existence of

---

[1] Addiction and Criminal Responsibility Stephen J. Morse, in Graham, George and Poland, Jeffrey Stephen (Eds.). *Philosophical Psycho-pathology: Addiction and Responsibility.* Cambridge, MA, USA: MIT Press, 2011.

[2] *Regulating tobacco,* R. L. Rabin & S. D. Sugarman (Eds.) Oxford U. P. , 2001.

[3] Viscusi (2002) *Smoke-filled rooms: A postmortem on the tobacco deal.* (U. of Chicago Press, p. 173)

the weight-loss industry attests. On the other hand, many smokers have quit and this point was made by one of the executives early in the discussion with Waxman's committee. If the browbeaten tobacco execs had been a bit less intimidated, when asked the question they could have responded with their own question: how many of you congresspersons used to smoke but no longer do? Given the date, the age of the committee members and the fine political tradition of the smoke-filled room, perhaps 50% would have had to raise their hands. Not addictive for them, then! I look at the legal implications of the addiction charge in Chapter 5.

Are there any benefits to smoking?

In 2013, the health case against smoking, especially cigarette smoking, is pretty conclusive, although Fisher's precise experiment has not been done, even in some country less fussy about human rights than the US and Europe. Nevertheless, a few puzzles remain. For example, obesity is a health risk and so is smoking. Yet obese smokers are if anything a little less at risk than non-obese[1]. If smoking is a health risk and risks are more or less additive as the models assume, how can this be? Should the government urge smokers to put on weight?!

Headlines in 2011 proclaimed that cigarette smoking is a risk factor for Alzheimer's disease. But it turns out that this is only true if studies with any funding link to the tobacco industry are excluded: "When all studies were considered together, the risk factor for developing AD from smoking was essentially neutral at a statistically insignificant 1.05."[2] Even when (supposedly biased) industry-related studies are excluded, the risk ratio is still only 1.72, below the usual plausibility threshold of 2.

The assumption that independent-of-industry studies are unbiased is of course no more certain than the assumption of pro-smoking bias in all industry-related studies. The bias against smoking in the large community of scientists whose research is funded by health-related agencies may be

---

[1] Anna Peeters, A., Barendregt, J. and Bonneux, L. (2002) Why don't smokers show an increased mortality risk with overweight? *Obesity Research*, 10, 1092–1093.

[2] http://www.sciencedaily.com/releases/2010/02/100201093039.htm

no less strong than the opposite bias amongst tobacco-funded researchers. And there is always room in the journals for another study showing a bad effect of smoking!

An interesting footnote to all this is that nicotine, the key addictive but non-carcinogenic, ingredient of tobacco smoke, apparently has beneficial effects on cognitive function in schizophrenic and Alzheimer's patients.[1]

A slew of recent studies have also shown pretty conclusively that smoking is associated with (those weasel words again!) reduced risk of Parkinson's disease: "We confirmed inverse associations between PD and smoking and found these to be generally stronger in current compared with former smokers; the associations were stronger in cohort than in case-control studies. We observed inverse trends with pack-years smoked at every age at onset except the very elderly (>75 years of age), and the reduction of risk lessened with years since quitting smoking."[2] In other words, not only were smokers less likely than non-smokers to get Parkinson's, the protection diminished for quitters as the years since they stopped smoking elapsed. A pretty conclusive 'plus' for smoking, no? Well, maybe, or maybe not. What these correlational data mean – whether or not the relation is causal (does smoking really protect you from PD?) or just an association, what the causal agent in tobacco smoke might be, whether PD is averted or just delayed – nobody yet knows.

Scientists have been studying the effects of tobacco smoke on animals for over one hundred years. In some respects the oldest studies are more credible than studies from recent decades because you can do actual experiments with animals – you don't have to rely on correlations – and smoking was not then as politicized as it is now. In the 1920s, for example, the era of prohibition, alcohol was the target of choice for politicians and activists. Loony claims like "progeny conceived during drunkenness is doomed to idiocy" were commonplace. In the 1990s,

---

[1] Psychiatry Grand Rounds "Nicotinic drug reaction: The two-sided blade of addictive risk and therapeutic potential." by Edward D. Levin, Ph.D. Duke University Medical Center, February 9, 2012.

[2] Beate Ritz, MD, PhD; Alberto Ascherio, MD, DrPH; Harvey Checkoway, PhD; Karen S. Marder, MD, MPH; Lorene M. Nelson, PhD; Walter A. Rocca, MD, MPH; G. Webster Ross, MD; Daniel Strickland, PhD; Stephen K. Van Den Eeden, PhD; Jay Gorell, MD Pooled Analysis of Tobacco Use and Risk of Parkinson Disease *Arch Neurol.* 2007; 64(7):990-997.

however, tobacco took the heat: "The truth is, that cigarettes are the single most dangerous consumer product ever sold," opined Representative Henry Waxman, chair of a House committee on the regulation of tobacco products in 1994.[1.]

Early in the 20th century, however, smoking was not a hot topic. One early animal study[2] looked at the effect of alcohol, nicotine, tobacco smoke and caffeine on the health and fecundity of white mice. They found that the 'tobacco fumed' mice were more fecund than untreated controls, despite being lighter and having greater infant mortality. 'Fuming' increased fertility, but at the cost of greater infant mortality, apparently. A later study[3] concluded that moderate doses of tobacco smoke have beneficial effects on both the reproduction and maze-running ability of white rats. Smoke makes rats smarter, apparently. Of course, we don't know the exact composition or dose of the 'fuming' but, as we'll see, the best studies on secondhand-smoke effects on humans are consistent with these conclusions.

Overall, the evidence is that smoking is risky but far from invariably lethal, nor is it entirely without objective benefit. Its subjective benefit is of course unquestionable. Some smokers may be afraid of the consequences of their habit but – they like to smoke. And for some it has proved helpful in their work. Writer Beryl Bainbridge, a lifelong heavy cigarette smoker, found when she tried to give it up that she could not write. She died at seventy-five of breast (not lung) cancer. Prolific writer, philosopher and mathematician Bertrand Russell was more fortunate. When asked about his favorite vices, he answered "Oh, tobacco, I smoke a pipe all day long when I'm not eating or sleeping." "Hasn't that shortened your life?" asked his interviewer. "Well, they used to say it would when I

---

[1] House of Representatives Committee on Energy and Commerce, Subcommittee on Health and the Environment, April 14, 1994.

[2] L. B. Nice: Comparative studies on the effects of alcohol, nicotine, tobacco smoke and caffeine on white mice. II. Effects of activity. *Jour. Exp. Zool.*, January, 1913,14,123-151.

[3] The effect of tobacco smoke on the growth and learning behavior of the albino rat and its progeny. Pechstein, L. A.; Reynolds, W. R. *Journal of Comparative Psychology,* Vol 24(3), Dec 1937, 459-469

first took to it, but I took to it first some seventy years ago, so it doesn't seem to have had a very great effect so far."[1]

So, smoking is not lethal, not (by most standards) morally defective, not addictive for most people, and may even have beneficial health as well as psychological effects. But it is risky for the smoker – and dangerous to others, isn't it? I look at the dangers of passive smoking in the next chapter.

[1] Check out the interview at http://www.youtube.com/watch?v=80oLTiVW_lc

LIFE
IS A KILLER
WE ALL GET A
LIFE TIME
There is only now
This is the case against the anti-smoking fanatics and the doctors + bossyboots etc. etc.
Who are busy trying their best to make everything DULLER

Chapter 3

The Perils of Passive Smoke

Surely smoking is dangerous not just to the smoker, but to others? My mother, who smoked all her life and died at the age of 96 always tried to disarm criticism by saying "But I don't inhale" – to which her children always responded by saying, "But we do, Mother." It is inconceivable to many that 'secondhand' smoke is essentially harmless.

Especially high anxiety is aroused by possible effects of smoking on children. A recent *TIME* magazine warned "Secondhand smoke exposure raises kindergartners' blood pressure"[1] in a story that got national attention. So, causation has been established! Did the researchers (a European group in Bern and Heidelberg)[2] repeat Fisher's hypothetical experiment with two groups of parents, randomly assigned to smoke or not from their children's conception on? Well no, of course not. The study, like thousands of others on this topic, was correlational. The researchers just looked at an existing population and did a lot of statistics. The distinction between correlation and causation, well known to statisticians and experimental scientists, is now essentially ignored – not just by the popular press, like *TIME*, but even by many researchers.

It is hard to write about a study like this without throwing up one's hands in despair. Basically, what these guys did was trawl through government data on more than 4000 children looking at everything they could think of and then analyzing the data to death until they found something publishable – like more bad news about smoking.

---

[1] *TIME*, Monday, January 10, 2011

[2] Determinants of Blood Pressure in Preschool Children: The Role of Parental Smoking. Simonetti et al. *Circulation*, Jan. 25, 2011.

What did they find, exactly? Well, apparently diastolic BP was "affected by" – "associated with" would be more accurate – gender, height, BMI, birth weight, and parental hypertension, but "significant correlates" of systolic BP were gender, height, BMI, birth weight, gestational hypertension, parental smoking, and parental hypertension. The individual correlations are essentially zero. For example, the correlation (R^2) between systolic BP and parental smoking is *.0025*, which is as close enough to zero to make no difference. But then the authors apply fancy statistics, like stepwise multiple linear regression, to come up with their headline conclusion: "The adjusted likelihood to be in the top 15% of systolic BP distribution was increased by 21% in children exposed to passive smoking." (Why top 15%, why not top 50%? or top 10%? Because these were not statistically significant, probably.)

But if the regression steps had been done in a different order; if the fact that all these risk factors are correlated with one another, if the probably non-linear nature of these interactions were known, if some measure were taken of the repeat-reliability of BP measures, if we knew the number of correlations they *failed* to find, if, and if…Even if all these things were known, in the absence of experiment, we would *still* not know if there is any real cause-effect relationship between parental smoking (not other parental habits or parental genes) and the blood pressure of young children.

Despite the basic flaws of the statistical/epidemiological method, an official report recently concluded that "In 2003, over 11,000 people in the UK are estimated to have died as a result of passive smoking."[1] The same report concluded that passive smoke also contributes to a wide range of childhood afflictions, from asthma and wheezing to sudden infant death. It relied for these dire conclusions on lengthy literature reviews[2]. These reviews, termed 'meta-analyses', describe no actual experiments, of course. They rely on combining together a number of correlational

---

[1] *Passive smoking and children*, March 2010, op. cit.; http://www.ncbi.nlm.nih.gov/pubmed/15741188

[2] A recent example is Prenatal and Passive Smoke Exposure and Incidence of Asthma and Wheeze: Systematic Review and Meta-analysis. *Pediatrics* 2012;129;735, Burke, Hannah et. al. Originally published online March 19, 2012;

studies, and studying the level of smoking byproducts, usually cotinine, in children's blood.

Cotinine is a derivative of nicotine. It is used as a biomarker to assess recent exposure to tobacco smoke. The usual presumption is that a high level of cotinine = high exposure to smoke = injurious effect of exposure to environmental tobacco smoke. One problem is that nicotine is not the actual carcinogen in tobacco smoke, as we'll see in Chapter 5. Indeed, nicotine by itself can have beneficial cognitive effects, as we saw in Chapter 2. Consequently, its biomarker may have little or nothing to do with the supposed ill-effects of ETS.

A second problem is that the correlations between estimates of ETS exposure and various ailments are rather weak. Typical risk ratios are all less than two, which is the usual criterion for a real effect, given the many, usually unknown and uncontrolled, differences between the parents of children exposed vs. not exposed to ETS. As we know, US smokers tend to be poorer and less healthy than non-smokers for sociological as well as medical reasons. These differences are as likely to contribute to the differences in their children's health as parental smoking.

And finally there is the 'file-drawer problem'. How many studies of the effect of parental smoking on children's health failed to find any effect? We don't know, because studies with negative results are almost never published. We know they exist, but we don't know how many there are. But their existence makes highly questionable the results of meta-analyses based (necessarily) only on published work.

Ill effects of ETS on children may be insignificant in practice, but they are highly significant politically. Since children have less control over their environment than adults, supposed ill-effects of ETS on children have been used to justify sweeping smoking restrictions.

After the uncertainty of correlational studies, I turn with some relief to an actual and very clever 'natural' experiment' on children and secondhand smoke[1]. The fact that some women, unable to conceive on their own, are now able to bring to birth eggs of another woman via In

---

[1] Disentangling prenatal and inherited influences in humans with an experimental design. Frances Rice, Gordon T. Harold, Jacky Boivin, Dale F. Hay, Marianne van den Breea, and Anita Thapar 2464–2467, *PNAS,* February 17, 2009, vol. 106 no. 7

vitro fertilization (IVF), makes it possible to separate genetic and environmental effects on the fetus. This study compared children born to smoking and non-smoking mothers and either genetically related to the mother or not (i.e., conceived via IVF). The idea was to separate the effects of genetic differences between mothers from the effects of their smoking habit. The 'test-tube' babies of the IVF mothers have nothing genetically in common with the mothers who give them birth. Consequently, by comparing these children with the children of similar women who conceived naturally, the authors were able to separately identify the effects of mothers' smoking habit.

The researchers looked at two things about these two groups of children: birth weight and, of more concern, antisocial behavior of the kids at around seven years of age, measured by a questionnaire given to the parents. They concluded "prenatal smoking reduces offspring birth weight in both unrelated and related offspring, consistent with effects arising through prenatal mechanisms independent of the relation between the maternal and offspring genomes. In contrast, the association between prenatal smoking and offspring antisocial behavior depended on inherited factors because association was only present in related mothers and offspring." In other words, in this 'natural experiment' the birth-weight effect is attributable to the mother's smoking, but the behavior problems of the child are genetic[1]. There are may be some effects of lower birth weight on health and behavior in later life, but they are of course very hard to measure and this study did not elaborate further on them.

The take-home from this study is that the few modest associations that have been reported between secondhand smoke and children's ailments are at least as likely to reflect genetic and other differences between smokers and non-smokers as causal effects of smoke.

Despite the scientific uncertainties, most people have no doubt that smoking injures non-smokers via secondhand smoke. Recent headlines proclaimed that a group at the Harvard Medical School has even found (actually, they just *assumed* – the study was in fact about people's beliefs

---

[1] Unfortunately, even some commentators who should know better still quote the spurious smoking-mother-violent-child link: Adrian Raine interview, 2013: http://www.scientificamerican.com/article.cfm?id=secrets-criminal-mind-adrian-raine&page=2

on the subject) that *third*-hand smoke, the residue on *smokers' clothes,* is a danger to children[1]! Here is what they say: "What's Known on This Subject: There is no safe level of exposure to tobacco smoke. Thirdhand smoke is residual tobacco smoke contamination that remains after the cigarette is extinguished. Children are uniquely susceptible to thirdhand smoke exposure." Not a shred of evidence is offered for these claims, published in a prestigious pediatric journal. All the authors can be sure of is that almost every reader will agree and no confirmation will be required.

"Well, here's another nice mess you've got us into!" as Hardy said to Laurel. The greatest statistician of the twentieth century was unconvinced 50 years ago by the even-then-considerable correlational evidence for health effects of "mainstream smoke" (MS). How much more difficult will it be to prove that environmental tobacco smoke is dangerous! ETS is after all lower in concentration than MS by a factor of 1000 or more. The proportion of time non-smokers are exposed to ETS is typically less than smokers' exposure to MS by a factor of at least 10, and perhaps 100 or more. The total risk – concentration times exposure – is likely to be thousands of times smaller than the danger posed by mainstream smoke which, nevertheless, has taken 50+ years of research to establish conclusively. A biomedical colleague of mine, expert in these matters, had a saying: "the solution to pollution is dilution": ETS is plenty diluted!

The Centers for Disease Control disagrees. Echoing the conclusion of the *709-page* 2006 Surgeon General report,[2] the CDC bluntly concludes: "There is no risk-free level of contact with secondhand smoke; even brief exposure can be harmful to health."[3] The number of pages in these reports is a tip-off to the rickety case they attempt to bolster. A handful of pages would suffice to present the evidence that *Plasmodium* causes malaria or

---

[1] Beliefs About the Health Effects of "Thirdhand" Smoke and Home Smoking Bans. Jonathan P. Winickoff, MD, MPH, Joan Friebely, EdD, Susanne E. Tanski, MD, Cheryl Sherroda, Georg E. Matt, PhD, Melbourne F. Hovell, PhD, MPH and Robert C. McMillen, PhD. *Pediatrics* Vol. 123 No. 1 January 2009, pp. e74-e79:

[2] The Health Consequences of Involuntary Exposure to Tobacco Smoke: A Report of the Surgeon General (2006) http://www.surgeongeneral.gov/library/secondhandsmoke/report/

[3] http://www.cdc.gov/tobacco/data_statistics/fact_sheets/secondhand_smoke/general_facts/

poor sanitation promotes cholera. Only if the argument is light does the report need to be heavy! The report's 'no risk-free level...' conclusion is simply astonishing. Can it be true? Can you even prove that there is *no* risk-free level?

No. It is almost certainly false. So why has it become the health-establishment consensus? The reason is that science is a social activity. What is accepted as truth is not a given, not guaranteed by the too-confidently named "scientific method." It depends in an additive sort of way on a balance of forces. In *experimental* science, causation *can* be established directly and irrefutably. If we think that A may cause B, we can manipulate A, turn it on and off, or apply A to one group and not-A to another, matched, group and see if the conditions/groups differ – and then (ideally) repeat (replicate). Hence Fisher's hypothetical experiment with the teenagers and smoking as the conclusive but unethical, hence un-doable, way to prove or disprove a causal link between smoking and disease. If an experiment can be done, and the results are clearcut, social factors have minimal effect. If you doubt a result, just repeat the experiment. The fact that one group – tobacco companies, or health-related or revenue-hungry government departments – has a vested interest in one outcome rather than the other has little effect, because the data are so compelling.

Not so when the question arouses passions and crucial experiments are impossible. Almost anything related to health raises fear, anxiety and even anger: "Let me tell you...about my dad's death from emphysema...Not one day went by when he didn't say 'I know these damned cigarettes are killing me, but I can't quit.'"[1]. Once suspicion is aroused, and the question is one about which people feel strongly, "don't know" is never an acceptable response. Even less acceptable is "can't know" which is probably the right response in the case of passive smoke whose long-delayed effects are either zero or very small.

The voices of smokers themselves are muted. Many are embarrassed by their habit, afraid of its effects, and would give up smoking if they could. Amazingly, there seems to be no pro-smoking (or at least 'anti anti-smoking') activist group in the US. (There is a small one in the UK

[1] Letter placed in the record of Waxman's 1994 congressional committee.

though[1].) Americans, as de Tocqueville, perceptive author of *Democracy in America* (1831) and in general pro-American, discovered nearly two centuries ago, can be surprisingly conformist: "I know of no country in which there is so little independence of mind and real freedom of discussion as in America."[2]. Despite our self-proclaimed reputation for rugged individualism, Americans in fact have a history of conformity almost as strong as their history of Puritanism. The two combine to form an anti-smoking majority, which tends to have the last word.

The tobacco companies have no principled position other than profit. Thus, neo-Puritan anti-smokers have the moral edge. Indeed they feel virtuous, smug even, about their assaults on smokers' rights. Like the Spanish Inquisition, they know it's for their victims' own good!

Public smoking policy in the US has a nefarious history that would put Somalia[3] to shame. As time has passed, the role of real science has declined – although the (supposedly) scientific page count continues to increase. The leading roles are played by politicians, but they are increasingly upstaged by the courts and anti-tobacco activists – see for example Michael Pertschuk's anti-smoking instruction manual *Smoke in their eyes: Lessons in movement leadership from the tobacco wars*.[4] Much money and passion are involved. Thus, few of the participants have behaved in a creditable way. We've already glimpsed the jaw-dropping evasiveness of the cigarette executives. Now see the arrogant know-it-allness of their opponents.

The data on health risks of passive smoking are incredibly weak. In 1998, Judge William L. Osteen, of the United States District Court for the Middle District of North Carolina, vacated the Environmental Protection

---

[1] From their web site: "Founded in 1979, Forest represents adults who choose to smoke tobacco and non-smoking adults who are tolerant of other people smoking. The group was set up by Sir Christopher Foxley-Norris, a former Battle of Britain fighter pilot. A lifelong pipe smoker who died in 2003 aged 86..." http://www.forestonline.org/output/Home.aspx There is a US website that presents pro-smoking material http://www.smokinglobby.com/ but there seems to be no formal organization associated with it.

[2] *Democracy in America*, Chapter 15.

[3] Number one in Forbes' list of corrupt nations http://www.forbes.com/2010/11/01/most-currupt-countries-2010-business-beltway-currupt-countries.html

[4] Vanderbilt University Press, 2001.

Agency's classification of secondhand smoke as a "known carcinogen." He concluded that the EPA had (for example) "cherry-picked" existing data. But his verdict could not long withstand the efforts of smoking opponents. The tobacco companies were subsequently convicted by another judge using RICO (The Racketeer Influenced and Corrupt Organizations Act) – a law written for John Gotti rather than the Marlboro Man. Judge Gladys Kessler, who has become a career opponent of tobacco, in effect reversed Judge Osteen's anti-EPA verdict. In a *1742*-page decision in 2006, in the D.C. District Court, she concluded that the tobacco companies were guilty of *racketeering* for asserting that secondhand smoke and low-tar-and-nicotine cigarettes have less toxic effects on human health than mainstream smoke from regular cigarettes. These are not outlandish claims by the tobacco companies. It is hard to see why they should be illegal.

Judge Kessler is worth quoting at length: "…this case is really about…an industry, and in particular these defendants, that survives, and profits, from selling a highly addictive product which causes diseases that lead to a staggering number of deaths per year, an immeasurable amount of human suffering…"

Let's just pause here and reflect on the judge's words. Certainly smokers who die of lung cancer and other smoking-related ills do suffer. But I'm afraid that dying is rarely a walk in the park for anyone, smoker or non-smoker. Is it worse for smokers? Possibly, but against their suffering, suffering which is shared with all mortals, must be balanced the harmless pleasure they get from their habit. Unlike many other pleasurable habits, like drinking alcohol, sexual promiscuity and taking drugs, smoking really is harmless to others. Neither the pleasure smokers get from their habit, nor the fact that we all die and suffer, weighed at all with Judge Kessler.

She continued "…human suffering and economic loss, and *a profound burden on our national health care system*. Defendants have known many of these facts for at least 50 years or more. Despite that knowledge, they have consistently, and repeatedly, and with enormous skill and sophistication, *denied these facts to the public*, to the Government, and to the public health community. [my emphasis]"

So the cigarette companies who, like every other company, sugar-coat their product, are somehow responsible for denying the public the knowledge that cigarettes are dangerous. This despite the fact that prominent health warnings had been on every cigarette packet for more than 40 years before her verdict! Bertrand Russell was warned of the dangers of smoking in the nineteenth century! As Alistair Cooke pointed out in 1954, the health risks of smoking have been well known at least since the famous "Cancer by the Carton" *Reader's Digest* piece in 1950. The slang term "cancer stick" has been in use at least since 1958[1]! Watson and Holmes joked about the ill-effects of tobacco smoke ("poisonous atmosphere" etc.) in the 1890s. To say that in 2006 any sentient American was ignorant of the dangers of smoking is beyond parody. Undeterred by these facts, an eminent lawyer who agrees with Judge Kessler, cheerfully refers to "racketeering defendants" with a "despicable history of... deadly misdeeds over half a century."[2]

And reflect a moment on the free-speech implications of the judge's charge that they have *denied these facts* ["addictive product," "staggering deaths," burden on health system, etc.] *to the public.* As we'll see, all of the judge's "facts" are questionable and at least one is false.

If these damning charges were all true, tobacco should surely be outlawed immediately! The main reason it is not I will take up in Chapter 6 in connection with the wondrous 1998 tobacco Master Settlement Agreement, which has been compared to the tacit alliance of Baptists and bootleggers during prohibition[3].

So, bearing in mind the Surgeon General's sweeping verdict – "There is no risk-free level of secondhand smoke..." – let's look at the best

[1] 1958 is the earliest reference for *cancer stick* listed in the *Oxford English Dictionary*.

[2] http://tobacco.neu.edu/litigation/cases/DOJ/kessler_decision_0806.htm. Mark Gottlieb, who writes thus immoderately, is Director of the Tobacco Products Liability Project at Northeastern University School of Law in Boston. He is presumably a scholar, dedicated to objectivity. In any event, he knows he's right.

[3] Bruce Yandle, Joseph A. Rotondi, Andrew P. Morriss, and Andrew Dorchak, Bootleggers, Baptists, and Televangelists: Regulating Tobacco by Litigation. *University of Illinois Law Review,* 4(2008): 1225-1284.

available data on the effects of passive smoking. In 1998 a *Wall Street Journal* column[1] concluded:

> ...it is now obvious that the health hazard of environmental tobacco smoke (ETS) has been knowingly overstated. The only large-scale definitive study on ETS was designed in 1988 by a WHO subgroup called the International Agency on Research on Cancer (IARC). It compared 650 lung-cancer patients with 1,542 healthy people in seven European countries. The results were expressed as "risk ratios," where the normal risk for a non-smoker of contracting lung cancer is set at one. Exposure to tobacco smoke in the home raised the risk to 1.16 and to smoke in the workplace to 1.17. This supposedly represents a 16% or 17% increase. But the admitted margin of error is so wide – 0.93 to 1.44 – that the true risk ratio could be less than one, making second-hand smoke a health benefit.

In other words, there is no real evidence for any effect of ETS on the incidence of lung cancer – the disease most closely tied to smoking. There are several other studies that are similarly inconclusive. A National Cancer Institute study in 1998 concluded "Our results indicate no association between childhood exposure to ETS and lung cancer risk. We did find weak evidence of a dose–response relationship between risk of lung cancer and exposure to spousal and workplace ETS. There was no detectable risk after cessation of exposure."[2] Little has changed since 1998 other than the decibel level of official warnings.

---

[1] *Wall Street Journal* - European Edition (March 12, 1998); See also Multicenter Case–Control Study of Exposure to Environmental Tobacco Smoke and Lung Cancer in Europe. Paolo Boffetta et al., *Journal of the National Cancer Institute*, Vol. 90, No. 19, October 7, 1998.

[2] See also Lies, damned lies, & 400,000 smoking-related deaths. Robert A Levy, Rosalind B Marimont. *Regulation*. Fall 1998. Vol. 21, Iss. 4; pg. 24, 6 pgs and an attempted rebuttal by two people from the American Council on Science and Health: Alicia M. Lukachko and Elizabeth M. Whelan. *Regulation*, 2000. Vol. 23, Iss. 1; pg. 2, 10 pgs.

The most extensive recent study[1] with any credibility looked at 35,000 never-smokers in California with spouses with known smoking habits. This reference appears in the citations for Chapter 7 of the 2006 Surgeon General's 709-page report, but is not discussed in the text. (Still cherry-picking, apparently!) Presumably these spouses of smokers had pretty much the maximum level of exposure to secondhand smoke – certainly much greater than the exposure of customers in bars and restaurants. The participants were selected from 118,000 adults enrolled in late 1959 in a cancer-prevention study. The numbers are large (good) and the researchers asked a simple question (better): are Californians who are married to smokers likely to die sooner than those married to non-smokers? Their answer is unequivocal:

> No significant associations were found for current or former exposure to environmental tobacco smoke before or after adjusting for seven confounders and before or after excluding participants with pre-existing disease. No significant associations were found during the shorter follow up periods of 1960-5, 1966-72, 1973-85, and 1973-98...The results do not support a causal relation between environmental tobacco smoke and tobacco related mortality, although they do not rule out a small effect. The association between exposure to environmental tobacco smoke and coronary heart disease and lung cancer may be considerably weaker than generally believed.

Again no, or little, effect of secondhand smoke. ETS exposure time for spouses will be much greater than for restaurant and bar patrons,

---

[1] Environmental tobacco smoke and tobacco related mortality in a prospective study of Californians, 1960-98. James E Enstrom, Geoffrey C Kabat, *BMJ* VOLUME 326 17 MAY 2003. See also Environmental Tobacco Smoke and Coronary Heart Disease Mortality in the United States—A Meta-Analysis and Critique. *Inhalation Toxicology*, 18:199–210, 2006. The *BMJ* paper produced a storm of criticism because it questioned the link between secondhand smoking and illness. Anyone who thinks that smoking is treated dispassionately by the medical community should take a look at these comments: BMJ, 15 May 2003. See also Geoffrey C Kabat *Hyping Health Risks: Environmental Hazards in Daily Life and the Science of Epidemiology*. Columbia University Press, 2008, for an extended discussion of ETS.

though perhaps comparable to the exposure of employees in smoking-permitted restaurants and bars. So this study is a relatively strong test of the lethality of ETS.

But surely there must be effects of ETS on things like bronchial conditions, asthma, etc.? Maybe, but testing for these relatively common minor effects is much more difficult than answering simpler questions about the association between ETS and death or lung cancer. The variability among diagnoses is larger, the incidence of these conditions in the absence of ETS is much higher, and the possibilities for bias much greater. If the patient's parent or spouse smokes, most physicians will readily make the 'smoking caused it' connection, for example, even in the absence of anything but the presenting symptom. Doctors are more likely to look for health problems, especially bronchial problems, in patients who have been exposed to tobacco smoke. Diagnosis of the condition itself is likely to be influenced by what the doctor knows of the patient's exposure to smoke.

The bottom line is that even with maximal exposure to ETS, evidence for serious health effects of ETS is minimal to zero. That's not to say that some studies haven't found small effects. A European study concluded[1]: "Our results indicate no association between childhood exposure to ETS and lung cancer risk. We did find weak evidence of a dose-response relationship between risk of lung cancer and exposure to spousal and workplace ETS. There was no detectable risk after cessation of exposure." But, given the veritable kaleidoscope of statistical techniques that have been applied to large amounts of rather dodgy data – usually ex-post-facto self-reports to a variety of questionnaires – and the tendency to stop once a significant result *has* been found, a few (one in 10 or more) significant results should be expected just by chance[2]. Under the normal rules of experimental science, this pattern of results would mean "no effect."

---

[1] Multicenter Case–Control Study of Exposure to Environmental Tobacco Smoke and Lung Cancer in Europe. Paolo Boffetta, et al. *Journal of the National Cancer Institute,* Vol. 90, No. 19, October 7, 1998.

[2] In a similar situation: "…as one National Institute of Environmental Health Sciences researcher puts it, asking for anonymity, "Investigators who find an effect get support, and investigators who don't find an effect don't get support. When times are tough it becomes extremely difficult for investigators to be objective." Epidemiology faces its limits. Gary Taubes *Science* 269, July 14, 1995: 164.

Certainly there is nothing – *nothing* – in the science to justify the massive interference with individual rights entailed by no-exception smoking bans. Richard Doll, the epidemiological pioneer who provided the first convincing evidence for the effect of cigarette smoking on lung cancer, said not long before his death at the age of 92, "The effects of other people smoking in my presence is so small it doesn't worry me."[1] So there is no evidence that workers in bars and restaurants are at risk from smokers. But many, scared out of their wits by a torrent of bad publicity, surely think they are. (One solution: hire only smokers for work in smoking-permitted establishments. I suspect there would be a flood of applicants!)

"No effect" of secondhand smoke should not surprise. The human race discovered fire, by the best estimates, some half a million years ago. The Franklin stove was invented in 1741. In between, human beings lived with smoke most of the time. In the winter, they heated their huts with open fires, which filled the air with wood smoke; they cooked with open fires all year round. It would be surprising if the human race had not developed some resistance to the potential ill effects of smoke.

[1] http://news.bbc.co.uk/2/hi/health/3826939.stm

Chapter 4

The Cost of Smoking

I have discussed the morality of smoking, its supposed lethality, its addictiveness and its effects on nonsmokers. The evidence shows that if smoking is a sin it's a pretty venial one; nor is smoking as lethal as its critics charge and many smokers imagine. The health effects of passive smoke are almost impossible to measure. The best attempts have mostly failed to find significant effects.

This chapter deals with the most serious policy-related charge against smoking: that it costs non-smokers money – smoking has a Public Cost. Smoking-related disease is "a profound burden on our national health care system." wrote Judge Kessler. As we've seen, the National Socialists agreed (all those lost Volkswagens). "Smoking imposes a huge economic burden on society—currently up to 15% of total healthcare costs in developed countries." says an article in the BMJ in 2004[1]. The case seems unarguable. A substantial fraction of smokers die of smoking-related illnesses. Treating illness, especially if the treatment is protracted and often ineffective, as it is with COPD[2] and many cancers, is always expensive.

But "obvious" is not always "correct." The smoking-costs-us folk seem to forget (brace yourself!) that we all die, even non-smokers. As the bumper sticker reminds us "Eat right, exercise – die anyway." The facts about the health-care cost of smoking are in fact the opposite of the common preconception. For the 24-50 age range, smokers cost a bit more, thereafter they cost quite a bit less because smokers die a bit earlier than non-smokers: Overall "smoking actually saved the Medicare program money,

---

[1] Economics of smoking cessation. Steve Parrott and Christine Godfrey. *BMJ* Volume 328 17 April 2004.

[2] Chronic Obstructive Pulmonary Disease – emphysema, chronic bronchitis.

$2,800 per male smoker aged 24 and $600 per female." concluded Sloan et al. from a database up to 2002.[1] Data gathered since, which I discuss at more length in a moment, confirm this conclusion: smokers save society on health-care costs.

What matters for the cost argument is the manner of our dying: when do we die? And how long and costly is the process? The cost-saving early death of smokers was pointed out by the defense – Philip Morris Co. – in a 1998 Minnesota case. Cleverly disparaged by the plaintiffs as the "death-credit" argument, relevant evidence was specifically excluded by the judge in the case. I return to the legal issues in later chapters.

The costs of health care for the elderly in the last years of life are always much the highest. One study, for example, found that "From 1992 to 1996, mean annual medical expenditures (1996 dollars) for persons aged 65 and older were $37,581 during the last year of life versus $7,365 for non-terminal years."[2] Hence, dying of an acute – brief – condition is usually less costly than hanging on with some disabling but eventually terminal ailment. As we saw with the two forms of malaria in Colombia, the more lethal, but rapidly fatal, form was less costly to the country than the less lethal, chronic form.

So it is with smoking. In the year 2000, Philip Morris, recognizing that it might not be considered the most credible investigator, asked the Arthur D. Little company to do a study for the Czech Republic on the cost to the *state* of smoking. The conclusion: smoking, because of early mortality and tax revenue, represents a net *benefit* amounting to about $1227 per smoker[3].

---

[1] Sloan, Frank A.; Ostermann, Jan; Conover, Christopher; Picone, Gabriel; Taylor, Jr., Donald H. (2011-08-08). *The Price of Smoking* (Kindle Locations 1971-1975). MIT Press. Kindle Edition.

[2] Medical Expenditures during the Last Year of Life: Findings from the 1992–1996 Medicare Current Beneficiary Survey Donald R Hoover, Stephen Crystal, Rizie Kumar, Usha Sambamoorthi, and Joel C Cantor *Health Serv Res*. 2002 December; 37(6): 1625–1642.

[3] Public Finance Balance of Smoking in the Czech Republic http://hspm.sph.sc.edu/courses/Econ/Classes/cbacea/czechsmokingcost.html

Anti-smoking activists expressed horror at this finding. One commented:[1]: "Even if it were true that smokers dying young would save money for the economy, it's a real scary logic on which to base policy". Well, yes – unless attacks on smokers are justified by faulty economics, to which accurate economics is the only adequate response. And yes, if the government were to use economic arguments to facilitate, mandate or otherwise *encourage* smoking. Logic played no part in this debate. The reaction to the Czech study was so violent, that Philip Morris felt it had to issue a groveling apology the next year. But no one found anything scientifically wrong with the study.

A 2008 study to which anti-smokers have not yet expressed horror – perhaps because it doesn't have "smoking" in the title – is by a group of Dutch investigators. This seems to be the best available study on the actual costs of smoking to society. The investigators' aim was to see "whether this risk factor [obesity or smoking] primarily causes relatively cheap lethal diseases or rather expensive chronic ones." The study compared obese people, smokers and what they term a "healthy-living" cohort. They conclude: "the high medical costs of smoking-related diseases are more than offset by lower survival of smokers." They used Dutch medical costs for their estimate, but since per-capita US medical costs are almost twice Dutch costs, their results are likely to apply even more strongly to the US.

Their conclusion is that although smokers have a shorter life expectancy than the other two groups (77.4 years vs. 79.9 for the obese and 84.4 for the healthy-livers, all at age 20), their lifetime health-care costs are in fact lower. In summary:

> In this study we have shown that, although obese people induce high medical costs during their lives, their lifetime health-care costs are lower than those of healthy-living people but **higher than those of smokers.... The underlying mechanism is that there is a substitution of inexpensive, lethal diseases toward**

[1] See, for example, http://edition.cnn.com/2001/BUSINESS/07/16/czech.morris/index.html

less lethal, and therefore more costly, diseases.[1] [Baal et al., 2008, my emphasis]

Dying young is always a cost to society. A family may be left bereft. Years of potentially productive life are lost (economists call this *opportunity cost*). Traffic deaths, gun deaths, deaths from hazardous activities such as rock-climbing and motorcycling and deaths from infectious disease in the prime of life, are especially costly to society at large. But the fact – discouraging for smokers but not necessarily for other people – is that smokers who die of smoking-related ailments die (from a cost point of view) at just about the right time, just after retirement age. The opportunity cost for society is minimal or even negative because age of death is around the time the smoker would have ceased productive work anyway and after his or her children are independent. (And their children's inheritance will probably be larger for than non-smokers', because they have not had as much of a chance to spend it down!).

Smokers may, as some critics argue, be less efficient than non-smokers while on the job – going outside for a drag rather than working, for example. But some of these costs are imposed by no-smoking rules, and they are counterbalanced by claims of many writers, artists and other brain workers that smoking helps them think. So any on-the-job effect of smoking is probably outweighed by the hard fact that smokers seem to *spend a larger fraction of their lives working – contributing to society – than non-smokers*.

OK, but why, if smokers incur lower lifetime medical costs, do health insurers require a higher premium from them? Good question, to which there are two answers, one relating to the actual costs borne by insurers, the other to 'what the market will bear.' First, the actual cost. Lifetime health cost, if we are to believe the van Baal et al. study, is lower for smokers than non-smokers. But smokers also get sick sooner and die a bit

[1] Lifetime medical costs of obesity: prevention no cure for increasing health expenditure. Pieter H. M. van Baal, Johan J. Polder, G. Ardine de Wit1, Rudolf T. Hoogenveen, Talitha L. Feenstra, Hendriek C. Boshuizen, Peter M. Engelfriet, Werner B. F. Brouwer PLoS Medicine | www.plosmedicine.org, February 2008 | Volume 5 | Issue 2 |. In 2013 van Baal saw no need to revise the conclusion of the study (van Baal, personal communication).

earlier (on average) than non-smokers. In other words, more of smokers' health-care cost is likely to be incurred before 65, the age at which they become eligible in the US for government aid through Medicare. But this is the bit that falls most heavily on a private health insurer[1]. In other words, for the private insurer – but not for society at large or for the government via Medicare – smokers cost more than non-smokers. For society and for the government, smokers cost less.

The market answer is simple. Smokers have been so successfully stigmatized, and falsehoods about their health-care costs are so widely accepted, that the insurance industry can extract additional premiums from them with little pushback. Smokers, in this area as in so many others, are if not willing, at least passive, victims.

In fact, insurers, like other businesses, are probably always guided more by a 'what the market will bear' strategy' when it will get them more return than simple cost-plus. Apple, in its fashionable heyday, for example, was able to extract profit margins of 40% or more. As evidence for similar thinking by insurers, consider a case where early demise should *save* smokers money: lifetime retirement annuities. Early death represents a benefit to issuers of lifetime annuities, so if economics – insurers' cost – ruled, smokers should be offered *lower* premiums for lifetime annuities. Have you seen any such offers? I have not. Not cost, but what the market will bear, sets these rates.

Before I leave the topic of cost, let me leave you with this thought from a recent book on the 'graying' of the developed world: "An aging world is an increasingly dependent world. It will demand that a growing proportion of the population devote their lives to the growing share of the people who need care".[2] Do you think that smokers exacerbate or mitigate this looming problem?

---

[1] See review in Sloan, Frank A.; Ostermann, Jan; Conover, Christopher; Picone, Gabriel; Taylor, Jr., Donald H. (2004) *The Price of Smoking* (Kindle Locations 1971-1975). MIT Press. Kindle Edition.

[2] *Shock of Gray: The Aging of the World's Population and how it pits Young against Old, Child against Parent, Worker against Boss, Company Against Rival and Nation against Nation.* By Ted C. Fishman, Scribner, New York, 2010. See also Ken Murray: Why Doctors Die Differently: Careers in medicine have taught them the limits of treatment and the need to plan for the end. *WSJ,* Feb. 25, 2012.

Each smoker's death, like any death, is a tragedy for the deceased's family and friends. But for the community as a whole grief may be muted, because smokers' deaths, on average, cost less than the deaths of non-smokers. And these are medical costs alone. The numbers do not take into account years of social-security and other pensions that need not be paid to deceased smokers, the huge tax revenues from cigarettes, or the massive hidden tax levied in the US by the tobacco MSA. All the evidence is that smokers are a good deal for society. Why, then, should so many governments now discourage smoking and penalize smokers?

Why indeed? But first let me review the argument so far.

Longevity: As I pointed out in Chapter 1, in biology, lifespan is subject to evolutionary pressures, just like any other characteristic. A short life works for mayflies, a very long one for Galapagos tortoises. Much the same seems to be true of human societies: the race is not always to the long-lived. The connection between average lifespan and either economic success (Botswana, Columbia) or persistence of the culture (Israeli Jews vs. Arabs), is rather weak. In terms of *public* good, therefore, a longer lifespan is not always better.

Longevity is not an unalloyed personal good either, as Swift's fictional Struldbruggs and the very real assisted-suicide movement show. The last years of many lives can be miserable. The manner of dying – brief or protracted – and quality of life in the time just before death – relatively healthy vs. mentally and/or physically impaired – is what matters most to most people. So also time of death: people want to live long enough to see their children grow and have children themselves, but beyond that many are less sure, especially if their old age is to be "under all the usual Disadvantages..." (When they *are* old of course, the picture may change again and the survival instinct may take over, no matter how awful life may have become[1].)

Values: Facts alone cannot be a guide to action. Facts can help us decide on the best way to achieve our goals; they cannot provide those goals. The belief that science – fact and reason – alone can guide action is a type of "is-ought" fallacy identified by the Scottish philosopher David Hume in

[1] Sandra Loh's father, mentally and physically impaired at 91 and a huge burden on her, nevertheless retained his will to live.

the eighteenth century[1]. Hume showed that no fact by itself should move us to action. To act requires not just factual information, which is all that science can provide, but a motive or value. Alas, many of our greatest popular science-is-a-guide-to-life writers seem not to grasp Hume's insight, perhaps because the values that guide them are so obviously correct (to them) that they don't see them as values at all.

Values enter in to public policy in two ways, *utilitarian* and *absolute*. By utilitarian, I simply mean that policy be guided by a set of agreed goals – life, liberty and the pursuit of happiness come to mind. In an ideal world, policies are then chosen so as to maximize these goals (I'm simplifying greatly, of course; more on this later.) An alternative is simply to live by absolute principles, even if they may occasionally lead to ends we might not prefer under normal circumstances.

For example, there is a contrived problem that academic ethicists pose to their students: A loose railroad wagon is running away down a track that divides into two. You have control of the switch. If you do nothing, the wagon will strike a group of children and kill them all, but if you push the switch, the wagon will be diverted and just kill a single workman on the other track. What should you do? The utilitarian answer is: press the switch, because fewer lives will then be lost. But the absolute principle "take no life" says "do nothing" so you don't yourself cause a death.

Interestingly, the massive flooding in the Mississippi valley in the Spring of 2011 posed a similar real-world problem for flood-control agencies. Should they do nothing, and allow large cities to be flooded, or open a few floodgates, sparing the cities but flooding rural areas that would otherwise have been safe? With little debate, the authorities opened the gates, even though people who had chosen to live in safe areas were now flooded. A utilitarian solution that minimized total suffering. But a decision that harmed people who would otherwise have been safe – and discounted entirely the prudent choices of those who would have remained dry had the gates been left shut.

There is no easy resolution of this kind of conundrum. But it does illustrate the problems for health policy posed by things like smoking. Discrimination against smokers cannot be justified on utilitarian grounds,

---

[1] For an entry discussion see http://en.wikipedia.org/wiki/David_Hume , and Staddon (2004), op. cit.

because smokers save society money, rather than the reverse. The *only* way that public-health-based attempts to suppress smoking can be justified is via a three absolutes: that longer life is always better; that the harmless pleasure – happiness – derived by the smoker is somehow illegitimate and counts for nothing; and that the state knows the citizen's private interest better than he does. As the late Baron Jay put it in the UK "in the case of nutrition and health, just as in the case of education, the gentleman in Whitehall really does know better what is good for people than the people know themselves."[1]

To paraphrase *The Economist* "It may be best to make a case for improving health [extending life] because it is a good thing in itself, rather than on the basis of presumed economic benefits that may not appear for generations." Maybe, but since life-extension itself is costly, in money and in reduced freedom for some, and has ambiguous implications for larger social goals – like 'fitness' of the culture – it's by no means clear that we should accept *The Economist's* position.

Do we really want an Eleventh Commandment along the lines of "Thou shalt not engage in any risky behavior, no matter how pleasing to thyself and harmless to others – especially smoking."? Because smokers apparently cost society less than non-smokers, and because longer life *per se* has an ambiguous relation to the long-term success of a society, there simply is no clear utilitarian basis for a *public* effort to suppress smoking. If you, a nonsmoker, are opposed to it, it's because you don't like it, not because it's bad for you.

Readers with a logical frame of mind might at this point object: "This public/private health business is all very well, but what about the handicapped, or old people, people past retirement, past the age where they represent a net benefit to society? You say the State should leave smokers alone because they tend to die after they have ceased to be useful, so why should we help senior citizens via Social Security, Medicare and so on, if they make no contribution?" This was indeed the point of view of Socialists, both National and Fabian, like George Bernard Shaw, in the 1930s, who thought that the old and useless should be painlessly euthanized[2].

[1] In Douglas Jay, *The Socialist Case,* Faber and Faber, London, 1937.
[2] "Sir, or madam, now will you be kind enough to justify your existence?" http://www.youtube.com/watch?v=7WBRjU9P5eo&feature=related

Vegetarian Shaw was probably being ironic, but the Nazis were in deadly earnest.[1]

This is not my view and the difference is this. Helping the old is a generally agreed absolute value in our society, but smoking is not yet universally condemned as a sin[2]. Helping the old conforms to our expressed beliefs but, as I've tried to show, suppressing smoking does not. Most importantly, help is something that most old people welcome: aid is not forced upon them. It is quite otherwise for smokers. To the extent that they are not victims of a sort of Stockholm syndrome that causes them to embrace their tormentors, smokers do not welcome the costs, restrictions and penalties to which they are subject. Absent a real common-good benefit, there is no reason at all to penalize smokers beyond normal live-and-let-live limitations that respect both the rights of smokers and the rights of people who are upset by tobacco smoke.

On the evidence I have cited, smoking seems to be good for society not bad. But, apart from the pleasure it provides, it surely is bad for some smokers and their loved ones. So it seems that the decision to smoke or not should be not society's but the smoker's. He (and they) must balance the pleasures of smoking against the risk and make up his own mind (to whatever extent he can, since cigarettes are addictive for some) whether he wishes to smoke or not.

But the state has – should have – no dog in this fight. All health problems are not *public* health problems. Smoking is a *private* health problem, not a public health problem. The take-home of this chapter is that we need

---

[1] Shaw and many in the US elite, such as Yale economist Irving Fisher, in the first half of the twentieth century used two kinds of social-cost argument to promote forced sterilization of individuals identified as mentally sub-normal. The arguments were first, eugenic – allowing sub-normals to breed would degrade the genetic stock; and second, cost – their offspring would become charges on the state. The US was in fact the first country to enact such laws, which were in effect in some states until as late as 1974. We seem to be following a similar elite wisdom by enforcing draconian penalties against smokers – but without even the cost rationale.

[2] To the extent that smoking is an inefficient a form of suicide, and given that suicide is illegal in most states, a ban on smoking can be considered as no more than the ban on suicide. The fact that smokers do not intend their own demise (*mens rea*), and that smoking is not lethal for most smokers, makes this an unsustainable argument, however. So far, no one has proposed to ban risky activities on this basis.

to recognize which health issues are public and which are private. Just because something, like smoking or drug use or sexual practices or handgun ownership, affects health doesn't automatically make it a *public* health problem. Unless the practice either injures others or violates an absolute to which we are *all* committed, unless it is a universal abomination, the state – our government – should stick to public health and leave private health alone.

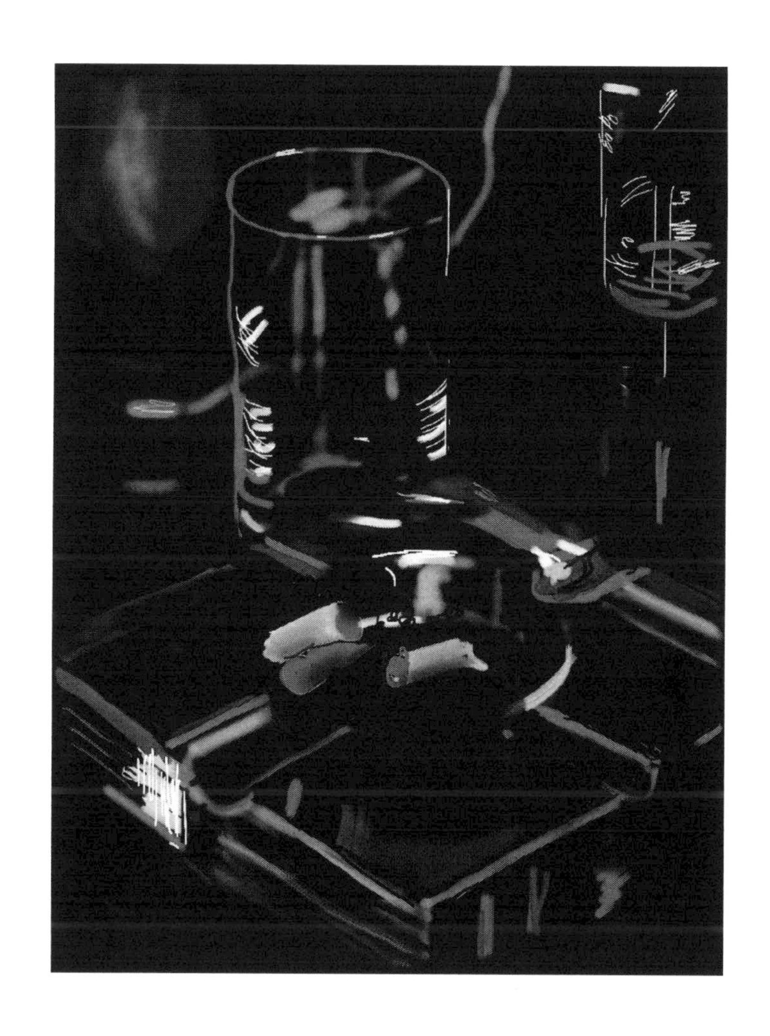

Chapter 5

The Law and Politics of Smoking

The birth of legislation is not a sight for the squeamish. Narrow self-interest, influential lobbyists, public prejudice and slippery rhetoric all combine to bring the squealing and often unsightly infant into the world. But, despite its messy origins, as the child grows into an adult, as new law works its way into action, all hope the result will, in the end, promote the common good. Quite often it does. But in the case of smoking and smoke-rs, it has not[1].

Previous chapters showed that smoking is not a public health problem. If anything, the common good is served by smokers: they contribute more in taxes, cost less in health care and may even spend a larger fraction of their lives in gainful employment, than the non-smoking population. Yet they are a despised group. The disrespect they suffer, the false belief that they cost the rest of society, and the very real distress of sick smokers, have all been exploited in numerous ways by the US legal system. Because smokers are stigmatized, they suffer under laws that would excite loud opposition if they applied to other "oppressed" groups. Because they are social pariahs, the states have been able to collude, in constitutionally questionable ways, to suppress competition among tobacco companies and extract huge financial contributions from smokers. This chapter and next describe how all this came about.

The modern history of tobacco regulation in the US is extraordinary. You really couldn't make it up. Here are the ingredients: money, sick

---

[1] My account of tobacco litigation and legislation has benefited greatly from Martha Derthick's excellent book *Up in smoke: Legislation to litigation in tobacco politics*. CQ Press, Washington DC, 2005 (2nd Ed.).

people, prejudice, law, money, asbestos, lawyers, medical advocates (one in particular), science, good and bad – and of course, *money*.

Asbestos: It all began with asbestos, which is an inexpensive naturally occurring fibrous mineral (a hydrated magnesium silicate, as we all know…). Asbestos is enormously useful. It has been used for generations in lamp wicks, as a joint compound, in woven form as a fabric, in hard sheets for roofing, as fireproof building insulation and for brake linings in vehicles. The twin towers might not have collapsed so soon on 9/11 had more of their steel been encased in asbestos rather than a less robust fireproofing material[1].

Asbestos is chemically rather inert (i.e., not poisonous) but occurs in a number of physical forms, some more toxic than others. There are straight and wavy asbestos fibers and the fibers are tiny – so tiny that they are easily inhaled and the straight ones, especially, easily penetrate the lung. So, workers long-exposed to asbestos dust and breathing asbestos fibers often get sick, primarily with asbestosis, a lung inflammation that shows up as chronic shortness of breath. These folk are also at increased risk of lung cancer and mesothelioma, a very nasty rare form, also associated with (those words again!) asbestosis.

Tort lawyers trawling for asbestos-linked mesothelioma cases still infest cable-TV advertising in the US, although those particular shoals are close to being fished out since many uses of asbestos were banned in the US in 1989[2]. The lawyers rely on the fact that the bad effects of asbestos are much delayed – it takes years of pretty heavy exposure to produce asbestosis, for example – and, in the case of cancer, rare – which makes proving causation especially difficult. The severity of the ailments and uncertainty about getting them conspire to cause chronic anxiety in people who have been exposed to asbestos, even asbestos in dustless form – solid sheets, for example – where the risk is negligible. Uncertainty about causation gives full scope to persuasive advocates.

---

[1] http://www.foxnews.com/story/2001/09/14/asbestos-could-have-saved-wtc-lives/

[2] Mesothelioma Doctors, Lawyers Join Hunt for Valuable Asbestos Cases. *WSJ* May 6, 2013. http://online.wsj.com/article/SB10001424127887324373204578374963941095622.html?mod=WSJ_hps_LEFTTopStories

> The cancer risk associated with asbestos dust has been long known: The cause of death, as determined at necropsy, is reported for 105 persons who had been employed at one asbestos works. Lung cancer was found in 18 instances, 15 times in association with asbestosis. All the subjects in whom both conditions were found had started employment in the industry before 1923 and had worked in the industry at least nine years before the regulations for the control of dust had become effective....From the data it can be concluded that lung cancer was a specific industrial hazard of certain asbestos workers and that the average risk among men employed for 20 or more years has been of the order of 10 times that experienced by the general population. The risk has become progressively less as the duration of employment under the old dusty conditions has decreased.

So wrote eminent English epidemiologist Richard Doll in 1955.[1] This study was followed by many others. Nevertheless, nearly twenty years later, the landmark 1973 ruling in the case of *Borel v. Fibreboard Paper Products Corp.* discounted common knowledge as something uncommon, at least to asbestos workers. Clarence Borel, the plaintiff, who died before trial, admitted that he knew asbestos was dangerous, but said he didn't know exactly how. The court decided that he had no obligation to find out, that it was the manufacturer's duty to warn of the health risk posed by exposure to asbestos dust, even though it was well known – at least in a general way – to any asbestos worker and had been for many years.

The opinion of Judge John Minor Wisdom had major effect, extending the doctrine of strict product liability to asbestos-related disease caused by insulation materials. In other words, asbestos became a 'defective product' for which the manufacturer was liable, even though its problems were intrinsic, well known, and not the result of manufacturing error. As a result, *Borel* provoked a vast expansion of asbestos litigation. No longer were sick workers limited by the provisions of workers' compensation. Ten years after *Borel* over sixteen thousand asbestos-related personal-injury cases had been filed in the US. Asbestos became the largest area of

---

[1] *Brit. J. industr. Med.*, 1955,12, 81. Mortality from lung cancer in asbestos workers. By Richard Doll

product-liability litigation[1] and more than 70 companies were forced into bankruptcy – including such well-known firms as Owens Corning Fiberglas and Kaiser Aluminum and Chemical.

The colorful heroes in this struggle to elevate provincial lawyers into the ranks of the super-rich were Richard "Dickie" Scruggs (best known saying: "We were so poor that if I hadn't been a boy, I wouldn't have had anything to play with.") in Pascagoula Mississippi, Peter Angelos in Baltimore, Ron Motley in Charleston, S.C. and Walter Umphrey in Beaumont Texas, plus a slew of minor characters. They did indeed become rich – on the order of tens of millions of dollars each. More importantly for the tobacco story, they acquired both the money and the expertise they needed to carry the product-liability argument to other areas – like guns and tobacco.

On to Tobacco: The ingredients of the strategy were straightforward: establish first that the product is harmful; second that the manufacturer knew this, *but concealed it*; third that users were ignorant of the harmful potential of the product; fourth that somebody (users, yes, but hopefully others as well) has suffered harm.

This strategy failed with guns (you mean guns are dangerous? Really!), but – amazingly in retrospect – worked fabulously well with tobacco. Tobacco added a couple of extra ingredients: not just harm, but *cost* – and not just cost to the individual, cost to the state. Meanwhile, the role of Greek chorus, singing distractingly but supportively in the background, was played by the FDA (federal Food and Drug Administration), conducted by anti-smoking crusader David Kessler, FDA commissioner from 1990 to 1997.

Dr. David Kessler (1951-) is a former New York pediatrician who also has a law degree. He became interested in regulatory legislation while a resident, when he also worked in the office of Senator Orrin Hatch. In 1990 he was appointed Commissioner of the FDA by the first President Bush. A new broom, he swept pretty clean, speeding up the drug-approvals process, tightening up labeling regulations and increasing the agency's efficiency.

---

[1] See, for example
http://www.crowell.com/documents/DOCASSOCFKTYPE_ARTICLES_424.pdf

But early in his tenure, Kessler became obsessed with tobacco and a tobacco industry he came to perceive as a knowing merchant of death. He put together a team of FBI-style investigators, recruited both from within and without the FDA, who reported directly to him. Their duties were to search out written records, public and confidential, to find and interrogate industry "moles," who were given James-Bond-like, usually tobacco-related, code-names like "Research"[1], "Macon," "Veritas" and "Philip," and to help Kessler put together his case for FDA regulation of tobacco.

The big deal, as Kessler saw it, was that nicotine is an addictive drug, cigarettes are therefore drug-delivery devices – and 'big tobacco' are bad people. They know what they are doing – it is a question of *intent*, which is the title of Kessler's blow-by-blow, date-by-date, name-by-name, and deception-by-deception (his as well as theirs) 492-page account of his (initially unsuccessful) attempt to place tobacco under the thumb of the FDA.[2]

Let's look at these three concepts: addiction, drug, and intent. What did Kessler mean by them? What did the law say about them? And what should we think?

Addiction and Responsibility: Dr. Kessler writes about addiction: "the word had acquired multiple meanings, signifying one thing to a scientist studying brain chemistry and another to a layman simply judging behavior." In fact the brain chemist can add little, because addiction has to do with conflicting goals. People are said to be 'addicted' when they want to do something, but it's bad for them – either in their own opinion or the opinion of others. Neither goals nor conflict are easily located in the brain or its chemicals. As I noted earlier "there is no consensual definition of 'addiction' within any of the specialty disciplines that study the condition, and there is no definitive biological marker for it."[3] Kessler in the end plumps for the layman's definition. Addiction is a bad habit that is im-

[1] AKA whistleblower Jeffrey Wigand, portrayed by Russell Crowe in the movie *The Insider,* which did not portray 'Big Tobacco' in a favorable light.

[2] *A question of intent,* David Kessler. New York, Public Affairs, 2001. Under the (irony drum-roll!) cigarette-smoking President Barack Obama, Congress again took up FDA regulation of tobacco in 2009.

[3] Stephen Morse, in Graham, George and Poland, Jeffrey Stephen (Eds.). *Philosophical Psychopathology: Addiction and Responsibility.* Cambridge, MA, USA: MIT Press, 2011, *op. cit.*

possible to give up. For him, the clincher was this: "After surgery for lung cancer, nearly 50% of those who survive resume smoking. Even when a smoker's larynx is removed, 40% start smoking again."[1] Yes, clearly for some people, smoking qualifies as addictive – although Kessler's example is not as convincing as he seems to believe. After all, for someone with incurable cancer, the horse has already left the barn. The cost of continuing to smoke may seem rather small when balanced against a quantum of solace during an otherwise bleak end of life.

Nevertheless, those 'big-tobacco' execs we saw in Chapter 2 denying under oath that nicotine is ever addictive were from one point of view quite accurate: nicotine by itself is not even pleasant, much less addictive, and cigarette smoking is not addictive for most people. I'll explain why in a moment. Nicotine is probably essential to the appeal of tobacco, but it is something about the whole smoking package, nicotine, tars, nitrosamines, etc., that makes it attractive. But the committee members in 1994 made no distinction between nicotine addiction and addiction to cigarettes. For example, committee member Bryant responded to one tobacco executive "Mr. Horrigan, it's very difficult for me to find you at this table characterizing anything as 'outrageous' after seven apparently intelligent people have stood here and told the American people, 250 million of which know better, that cigarettes are not addictive! What could be more ridiculous!"[2] For the committee members and for the surgeon general, even in his most recent (2010) report[3], tobacco is addictive and nicotine is the reason.

The psychopharmacological reasons for the effects of tobacco are not critical for the policy issues that are the focus of this book. The politico-legal issue is behavioral – are smokers responsible for their habit or not? – not physiological. I'll show how this works in a moment. But the addiction issue is an interesting illustration of the way that political bias enters into supposedly scientific judgments about smoking. In a highly critical 2011 review with the telling title *If the data contradict the theory, throw*

[1] AQoI, p. 120.

[2] Waxman Committee, April 14, 1994.

[3] US Department of Health and Human Services: How tobacco causes disease: the biology and behavioral basis for smoking-attributable disease: a report of the Surgeon General. Atlanta, GA, US Department of Health and Human Services, Centers for Disease Control and Prevention, National Center for Chronic Disease Prevention and Health Promotion, Office on Smoking and Health; 2010.

out the data: nicotine addiction in the 2010 report of the surgeon general, two researchers conclude: "...the nicotine addiction model presented in [the Surgeon General's Report] this chapter, which closely resembles its 22 years old predecessor, could *only be sustained by systematically ignoring all contradictory evidence*. As a result, the present SG's chapter on nicotine addiction, which purportedly 'documents how nicotine compares with heroin and cocaine in its hold on users and its effects on the brain,' is remarkably biased and misleading."[1] (my italics) Smoking may be addictive for a very few, but nicotine *per se* is not the reason.

So the tobacco executives were not without reasons for what looks like an absurd denial – and I will try to show that a more rigorous definition of addiction in fact excludes most smokers. So how did the execs defend themselves? In a word: poorly. "There is no intoxication" said one – although "intoxication" is not the point. Not all intoxicants are habit-forming and not all habit-formers are intoxicating. He could have made the argument that *pure* nicotine, whether inhaled or delivered by some other means, is not even pleasant. So how can it be addictive? Just like alcohol, the admixture with other ingredients makes a big difference. Not many drinkers prefer pure grain alcohol to malt whisky or VSOP cognac. Clearly, it's something about the whole nicotine+ package that smokers find attractive. Indeed, until they stopped for fear of legal repercussions, the tobacco companies did much research to try and find out just what the magic mixture was[2]. And finally, addiction to cigarettes falls on a spectrum of addictions: less bad (one presumes) than addiction to heroin or alcohol, worse than addiction to chocolate or ice cream.

Why does *addiction* even matter? Because of the *assumption of risk* defense in the law of torts. A plaintiff is barred from recovery against a negligent tortfeasor (causer of harm) if the defendant can show that the plaintiff *voluntarily* and *knowingly* assumed the risks associated with the relevant activity. If smokers both know that smoking is dangerous and choose voluntarily to smoke – if they are responsible for their own smoking behavior – then the cigarette manufacturer cannot be convicted of

---

[1] H. Frenk and R. Dar If the data contradict the theory, throw out the data: Nicotine addiction in the 2010 report of the Surgeon General. *Harm Reduction Journal* 2011, 8:12 http://www.harmreductionjournal.com/content/8/1/12

[2] See Derthick (2005) and Sullum (1998), op. cit.

causing harm. Otherwise, gun manufacturers could be sued for every gun death and cutlery manufacturers for every knife cut. But if smoking is involuntary, if smokers can't help it, then...

Do smokers know that smoking is risky? In fact, the evidence that smokers know, and even exaggerate, the risk of smoking – and have done so for years – is overwhelming, as I pointed out earlier. Not all agree, though. Tobacco opponent John Slade calls Viscusi's[1] theory "superficially appealing" and goes on to comment that even though you may know of a risk "it is quite another thing to feel personally vulnerable..."[2] Decision theorist Paul Slovic raised a similar objection[3]. More on this issue later.

Can smokers help smoking? Early on, juries invariably judged that smokers are responsible for their habit and repeatedly sided with the tobacco companies in suits brought against them by sick smokers. But addicts, by definition, cannot voluntarily choose, so responsibility shifts from them to whomever supplies their 'fix.' If that someone has deep pockets, the ambitious trial lawyer is off to the races: doing well by doing good. Addiction is the key that unlocked legal liability of the tobacco companies.

So is cigarette smoking truly addictive? Depends who you ask, and when. Before 1964, even the Surgeon General of the United States – an office subsequently held by increasingly Talibanic opponents of smoking – designated smoking a "habit" *not* an addiction[4]. But truth evolves in such matters. Before 1973, the *Diagnostic and Statistical Manual of Mental Disorders* (DSM III) of the American Psychiatric Association, bible of psychiatric diagnosis, regarded homosexuality as a mental disorder; afterwards it became a Sexual Orientation Disturbance and it vanished entirely from DSM IV. And smoking, initially just a habit, was replaced in DSM IV by something called "Tobacco Use Disorder" and "nicotine dependence". So by 2000 smoking had become a psychiatric problem. The

---

[1] Viscusi, W. K. (2002) *Smoke-filled rooms: A postmortem on the tobacco deal.* U. of Chicago Press.

[2] Marketing policies. In *Regulating tobacco,* R. L. Rabin & S. D. Sugarman (Eds.) Oxford U.P., 2001, p. 74.

[3] Paul Slovic, The perils of Viscusi's analyses of smoking risk perceptions. *Journal of Behavioral Decision Making,* 13: 273-6. 2000.

[4] Viscusi, W. K. (2002) *Smoke-filled rooms: A postmortem on the tobacco deal.* U. of Chicago Press.

DSM has come under increasing attack in recent years[1]. But a decade or two ago, it had more influence than its scientific credentials warrant. Nevertheless, after the watershed 1994 debacle in front of Henry Waxman's congressional committee, and aided by the addiction charge to shift legal blame from the smoker to the cigarette company, cigarette smoking has increasingly been seen as a largely involuntary activity 'enabled' by Big Tobacco for crass commercial gain.

What is the truth? "Truth was an early victim in the battle against tobacco" is the comment of one review, referring to the still-repeated claim that smoking 'causes 400,000 deaths' each year.[2] The simplistic claim that smokers are addicts is another and possibly even more pernicious falsehood.

There are in fact two kinds of bad effect of an addictive drug other than its possible effects on health. One concerns the common good: Addicts do bad things – can't hold down a job, commit crimes to feed their habit, get drunk and beat up their families or kill people with their cars. In short, addiction may have social costs that go beyond the addict. Some of this malfeasance can be traced to legal prohibitions – illegal drugs cost

---

[1] RL Spitzer *Am J Psychiatry* 1981; 38:210-215. DSM is not a scientific classification: "The strength of each of the editions of DSM has been 'reliability' – each edition has ensured that clinicians use the same terms in the same ways. The weakness is its lack of validity. Unlike our definitions of ischemic heart disease, lymphoma, or AIDS, the DSM diagnoses are based on a consensus about clusters of clinical symptoms, not any objective laboratory measure. In the rest of medicine, this would be equivalent to creating diagnostic systems based on the nature of chest pain or the quality of fever." From the National Institutes of Health website, April 29, 2013. http://www.nimh.nih.gov/about/director/2013/transforming-diagnosis.shtml
See also http://www.nytimes.com/2013/05/07/health/psychiatrys-new-guide-falls-short-experts-say.html?ref=health&_r=1&
And for a lighter take: DSM-5 Task Force Proposes Controversial Diagnosis for Dishonest Scientists. Matthew J. Gullo and John G. O'Gorman (2012) *Perspectives on Psychological Science,* 7(6) 689

[2] Lies, damned lies, & 400,000 smoking-related deaths. Robert A Levy, Rosalind B Marimont. *Regulation*. Washington: Fall 1998. Vol. 21, Iss. 4; pg. 24, 6 pgs. The exaggeration continues unabated. Each year the lethality of smoking seems to increase. By 2012, the *Financial Times* is reporting that "About half of all regular cigarette users eventually die of a smoking-related illness." (the actual figure is 20 to 25%) and not 6-8 but 16 years of life will be lost by smokers (Tobacco companies versus the plain truth. By Michael Skapinker, *FT*, May 15, 2012.)

more than they would if they were legal; hence 'controlled substance' addicts, already committing one crime by buying the stuff, will often commit a second to pay for what to them is an essential. But some bad effects are intrinsic.

The other aspect is private: too much alcohol always impairs judgment; opium is always enervating, and so on. On the other hand, many people drink responsibly and, in past times when many drugs that are now verboten were perfectly legal, many addicts managed to lead productive lives. Opium and its derivatives were used by Samuel Taylor Coleridge, Edgar Allan Poe, Charles Dickens, the emperor Marcus Aurelius and the saintly nurse Florence Nightingale, not to mention numerous modern celebrities and rock stars. Many have been damaged by their drug habits, but many have not.

But *none* of this bad stuff, public or private, is true of smoking 'addicts' – no violence, no enervation, no mental confusion. Healthy smokers lead productive lives. As I pointed out earlier, in the past many eminent men, from Winston Churchill, and FDR through Deng Xiaoping, were happy to be seen smoking. The addiction charge cannot, therefore, rest on cognitive impairment or the socially undesirable behavior of smokers. The claim must be that smoking somehow erodes smokers' will power, and so forces them to engage in life-threatening behavior. They smoke because they cannot help it and smoking kills them. The vendors, 'Big Tobacco,' are thus merchants of death.

Of course, smokers *could* help it the very first time. The decision to *begin* smoking is surely entirely voluntary. Hence David Kessler's logical, and politically savvy, efforts to suppress cigarette advertising and keep cigarettes out of the hands of children. Kessler assumed that adults, wiser and with more self-control, are less likely than children to begin smoking, hence less likely to be hooked. Unfortunately, there is some recent evidence that even this assumption may not be true:

> [T]he 1994 Surgeon General's report concluded that if adolescents can reach the age of 18 without smoking or using other tobacco products, their likelihood of beginning to do so is relatively small. There is some evidence, however, that this may be changing due to tobacco industry's targeting of young adults. Rates of smoking

have increased among college students, and there is evidence of initiation in this population as well..."[1]

This article blames advertising and promotion by the tobacco industry, a convenient target, for adolescent smoking. But that charge is nonsense. Marijuana, a controlled (i.e., illegal[2]) substance probably less addictive than tobacco, is nevertheless America's fourth largest cash crop, and number one in several states – without any advertising at all[3]. Who is to say, therefore – as the article implies – that people have zero tendency to begin smoking in the absence of advertising? Moreover, speaking as someone used to training animals, non-exposure may actually be a rather bad idea. Dogs like to chase cats. Keeping them away from cats doesn't help. The first time they see a cat, off they go. The only way to prevent chasing is to expose them to cats and train them *not* to chase. So it may be with tobacco. If you want your kid not to smoke, perhaps it is better let him actively learn to avoid it. A particularly ludicrous example of "If they don't see it they won't want to do it" is the move by the City of Liverpool in England to bar under-18s from movies that show smoking[4]. Does anyone with an above-room-temperature IQ really think that this will make smoking *less* attractive to teenagers?

So we are left with tobacco, or nicotine, 'addiction' as loss of self control by long-time smokers. Addicts (the argument goes) have diminished responsibility. Responsibility is the key. If smokers are not responsible for their habit, the doors to litigation open wide as blame shifts away from them to deep-pocketed tobacco companies.

Responsibility and the Insanity Defense: Personal responsibility is a concept central to something not obviously related to addiction, namely the legal *insanity defense*. The insanity defense is sometimes used to exonerate the perpetrator of a (usually violent) crime. The case of origin is

---

[1] Prediction of adult-onset smoking initiation among US air force recruits using the Pierce Susceptibility Questionnaire. *American Journal of Preventive Medicine,* Volume 28, Issue 5, Pages 424-429. C. Haddock, H Lando, S. Pyle, M. Debon, M. Weg, R. Klesges, A. Peterson, G. Relyea

[2] In most states.

[3] http://norml.org/index.cfm?Group_ID=4444. Admittedly, since growing marijuana is mostly illegal, exact figures are hard to come by – but you get the idea.

[4] London, *Daily Telegraph*, August 11, 2009.

the 19th century murder in England by one Daniel M'Naghten of Edward Drummond, secretary to Sir Robert Peel, the British Prime Minister and M'Naghten's intended victim. M'Naghten said that his mission was guided by the "voice of God". He was found not guilty by reason of insanity and his trial yielded the *M'Naghten Rule*: insanity is proved if the defendant was "labouring under such a defect of reason, from disease of the mind, as not to know the nature and quality of the act he was doing; or if he did know it, that he did not know he was doing what was wrong."

How does this work for smoking addiction? Smokers, at least those who sincerely want to quit, do of course know "the nature and quality of the act" and that smoking is "wrong" in the sense that it is risky. Where they resemble M'Naghten is that they do the act anyway. It is interesting, therefore, that a test for personal responsibility that I proposed some years ago[1] applies as well to smoking addiction as to the insanity defense.

Take M'Naghten first. Suppose, as M'Naghten pointed his gun at his intended victim, an authoritative prognosticating angel had whispered a warning in his ear: "You will be caught and hanged if you shoot" – would he still have pulled the trigger? Probably yes – he was obeying the voice of God, after all. Verdict: not responsible – insane. In contrast, consider the famous California case of the two Menendez brothers who, in 1989 murdered both their wealthy parents in an unprovoked attack. Their lawyers also tried the insanity defense, based on the supposed disabling effects of an alleged history of child abuse.[2] What would *they* have done in response to the informing angel? They would certainly *not* have continued, since they were after their parents' money, attempted to conceal their crime and went on a spending spree as soon as they could after their parents' murder. In short, they did the crime because they thought they wouldn't do the time. Verdict: responsible and therefore guilty. After two hung juries, the brothers were eventually both convicted. The real mean-

---

[1] Staddon, J. (1995) On responsibility and punishment. *The Atlantic Monthly,* Feb., 88-94: http://dukespace.lib.duke.edu/dspace/handle/10161/5944; Staddon, J. (1999) On responsibility in science and law. *Social Philosophy and Policy, 16,* 146-174. Reprinted in *Responsibility*. E. F. Paul, F. D. Miller, & J. Paul (eds.), 1999. Cambridge University Press, pp. 146-174.
http://dukespace.lib.duke.edu/dspace/handle/10161/3392

[2] The case is ably discussed in Dershowitz, A. (1994) *The abuse excuse*. Boston: Little, Brown.

ing of responsibility is normal sensitivity to the consequences of one's actions. Drummond fails that test, the Menendez brothers do not.

Now consider a comparable story for the smoking 'addict.' In the developed world, only about 25% of smokers die of smoking-related disease. Let us assume for the sake of argument that genetic science has advanced to the point that a DNA test can tell with 100% accuracy whether you will get lung cancer from smoking and when it will happen. What will the committed smoker do if given the bad news: yes, you will get cancer within the next five years unless you stop smoking? My guess is that close to 100% of smoking 'addicts' would in fact quit under such conditions. Verdict: responsible; smoking is their fault, no blame need attach to the cigarette company.

But what if the time delay is not five years but 30? What if the future cancer is not certain but just probable – conditions now, in the absence of the magic-gene analysis? Will the response change? Who is responsible then? Economics Nobelist Gary Becker has argued (with the aid of some clever math) that a case like this qualifies as *rational addiction*.[1] The smoker is simply balancing the delayed, hence discounted, cost of uncertain cancer against the present and future pleasures of smoking. The contribution of addiction is that these pleasures have been increased by past indulgence, a kind of long-term *l'appétit vient en mangeant.* To the extent that Becker is right and the behavior rational, the smoker still retains responsibility.

But imminence – the 5-year cancer horizon – is probably crucial. It is only that tiny fraction of smokers who would accept the certainty of imminent cancer rather than quit smoking who are truly addicted. These people alone can be absolved of legal responsibility for their own risky behavior.[2] But identifying them is an insuperable problem. Smokers cannot now be confronted with such a choice because the necessary knowledge is lacking – the question is entirely hypothetical. Also, in a legal wrangle, we cannot trust a plaintiff to respond honestly if (a) his answer

---

[1] Becker, G. S., & Murphy, K. M. (1988) A theory of rational addiction. *Journal of Political Economy, 96*(4), 675-700.

[2] For a book-length treatment that comes to much the same conclusion about addiction in general, see *Addiction: A Disorder of Choice*. Gene M. Heyman, Harvard U.P, 2009.

cannot be verified (he's telling us what he would do under entirely hypothetical conditions); and (b) large financial rewards depend on what he says. When presented with the possibility of a large monetary tort award, how many smoker plaintiffs will fail to affirm their willingness to continue smoking in face of certain death? How can we know if they are telling the truth?

In practice, the jury must decide based on a general understanding of human nature, rather than the details of any particular case. Judging the matter in this way, my guess is that the vast majority of smokers are indeed responsible for their habit. Until the late 1990s, US juries. and most of the public, agreed. As recently as 1997 "Polls ...showed that respondents by large margins believed that the cigarette companies should not be held legally or financially responsible for smokers' illnesses."[1]. Smoking-caused illness was the responsibility of the smoker not the manufacturer. But as the anti-tobacco lawyers re-armed and anti-smoking propaganda flooded the media, juries, and the public, changed their opinion.

There is another common-good issue raised by the addiction question, namely the collective effect of absolving any group of people of responsibility for their actions. If we assume that no smoker is responsible for his smoking, the incentives for those who are, who could give up if they wanted, are much reduced. If we think smoking is bad and we want smokers to quit, then absolving all smokers of responsibility, even those who could quit if they wanted to, is obviously a bad idea.

Kessler's two other issues were the status of nicotine as a drug and the tobacco companies alleged intent to manipulate it.

What is a *drug*? If nicotine is a "drug," tobacco automatically falls under the aegis of the FDA – so reasoned Kessler in 1991. Unfortunately tobacco is not mentioned in the act establishing the FDA because in 1938 no one thought of it as a drug. It is specifically excluded in Chapter II, Sec. 201 of the 2004 revision under "dietary supplements": "The term 'dietary supplement' – (1) means a product (*other than tobacco*) intended to supplement the diet..."[2] (my italics) On the other hand, nicotine surely is a drug if "drug" is defined as an article "(other than food) intended to

---

[1] Martha Derthick (2002) *Up in Smoke*. CQ Press, p. 132.

[2] http://www.fda.gov/opacom/laws/fdcact/fdcact1.htm

affect the structure or any function of the body of man or other animals" as specified in the Act. This is a very broad, probably too broad, definition. Essentially anything qualifies that affects human physiology but isn't food, from crack to dietary fiber – and that's anything of commercial or human interest. After all no one cares about, no manufacturer would make, and no user would ingest, smoke or otherwise absorb, a substance that had *no* effect on "the structure or ... function of the body." It's hard to see how anything at all is excluded by this definition.

The FDA Act is therefore contradictory, and the proper solution would have been a suitable amendment. But Kessler was not willing to wait on legislative action. He hoped to extend the reach of the FDA by focusing on the "drug" aspect. What if the tobacco companies *treat* nicotine like a drug? What if they explicitly manipulate the nicotine content of tobacco? "They treat nicotine just like sugar in candy" says one critic quoted by Kessler. On the face of it, that should not shock us: cigarettes are a taste-based product. If nicotine is critical to taste, why should the tobacco companies *not* manipulate it?

Here Kessler's argument gets a little muddy. First, he doesn't see "drug" quite as I have presented it. Even though he repeatedly quotes the FDA definition, "drug" for Kessler has quasi-medical overtones – it's like morphine or diazepam, not sugar or fiber, even though they also "affect the structure or ... function of the body." Second, he seems to think that an intent to manipulate, combined with addictive properties of nicotine, together prove his case that nicotine is a drug and weaken the 2004 Act's express exclusion of tobacco.

The Attack on 'Big Tobacco': In any case, *intended to affect* became the harpoon with which Kessler sought to pierce the heart of the tobacco industry. His persistent sleuthing in service of this aim soon began to pay off. At first he got a few hints that the tobacco companies were 'spiking' tobacco with the addictive ingredient, nicotine. This turned out not to be true, but he found out that the tobacco companies *were* experimenting with high-nicotine genetic variants of the tobacco plant and apparently committing minor illegalities in the process. In the course of these investigations, which involved 'sting' operations and secret testimony from dozens of disaffected tobacco ex-employees, thousands of pages of 'big tobacco's' confidential documents came to light.

They revealed a sort of schizophrenia in the industry. On the one hand, by their private behavior – covert research partly intended to lead to a 'safe' cigarette, internal memos affirming the addictive properties of nicotine – they seemed to be guilty of the sins asserted by Kessler: they knew that nicotine was the addictive ingredient in tobacco and they knew that smoking can cause lung cancer. On the other hand, by their public behavior – reluctance to acknowledge the dangers of cigarettes and, until relatively recently, complete denial of their addictive properties – they claimed to be unaware of any real downside to cigarette smoking. It was this schizophrenia – or duplicity – combined with the usual amoral desire of many successful business people just to get on with making money while obeying the letter of the law, that led to the downfall of…not the tobacco companies, actually, but the truly innocent victims: smokers.

What did the tobacco companies know of the dangers of cigarette smoking? Quite a bit, it turned out. The move to low-tar cigarettes reflects their awareness that the non-nicotine ingredients in mainstream tobacco smoke seem to be the main carcinogens[1]. A definitive independent review says bluntly[2]: "Nicotine is addictive and toxic, but it is not carcinogenic." Doubts have since been raised about the addictiveness of pure nicotine, but its carcinogenic effects do seem to be minimal. Even though a few studies *in vitro* and with mice have found some possibly carcinogenic effects[3], the nicotine in tobacco is not, apparently, the main health problem – it's the other stuff, tars, nitrosamines, etc.

Increasing the nicotine content of cigarettes may not be a bad idea, in fact. Heavy smokers smoke so as to maintain a roughly constant level of nicotine in their blood. So it doesn't actually matter whether they smoke

---

[1] Tobacco smoke carcinogens and lung cancer. Stephen S. Hecht *Journal of the National Cancer Institute*, Vol. 91, No. 14, July 21, 1999.

[2] Tobacco carcinogens, their biomarkers and tobacco-induced cancer. Stephen S. Hecht *Nature Reviews | Cancer* VOLUME 3 | OCTOBER 2003 | 733. http://www.nature.com/nrc/journal/v3/n10/abs/nrc1190.html

[3] Genotoxic and antiapoptotic effect of nicotine on human gingival fibroblasts. Gabriella Argentin, and Rosadele Cicchetti *Toxicological Sciences* 79, 75–81 (2004); Nicotine promotes colon tumor growth and angiogenesis through b-adrenergic activation. Helen Pui Shan Wong, et al. *Toxicological Sciences* 97(2), 279–287 (2007); Nicotine: potentially a multifunctional carcinogen? J. A. Campain *Toxicological Sciences* 79, 1–3 (2004)

high- or low-nicotine, high- or low-tar, "light" or heavy, filtered or unfiltered cigarettes. All are smoked with a frequency and intensity adjusted by the smoker to yield roughly the same blood-nicotine level.[1] But this means that low-nicotine cigarettes actually cause smokers to breathe in *more non*-nicotine – carcinogenic – ingredients: "Significant increases in terms of total volume of smoke inhaled and exposures to 'tar', nicotine, and lung carcinogens were measured (2- to 4-fold) and, because of smokers' compensation for low nicotine delivery, much greater overall exposure resulted from smoking low-nicotine cigarettes."[2] So, low-nicotine cigarettes cause smokers to take in more bad stuff, because they smoke more so as to maintain their nicotine intake roughly constant. If this is correct – and everything we know about the homeostatic (regulatory) properties of motivational systems suggests that it is[3] – then the tobacco companies were doing a good thing, not a bad thing (as Kessler claimed), by attempting to increase nicotine level in cigarettes. The richer the nicotine content, the less you smoke – and the fewer (non-nicotine) carcinogens you inhale.

As the legal battle began to heat up, the tobacco companies stopped research on a 'safer' cigarette, presumably at the behest of their lawyers who wanted to expunge all evidence that the companies were aware of, and acted upon, their knowledge of the dangers of cigarette smoking. The attempted cover-up backfired, big-time. As a result of Kessler's inquires, the trolling of Dickie Scruggs, of Marc Edell, plaintiff's lawyer in the landmark *Cipollone* case[4] (1988), and of other tort lawyers with anti-

---

[1] Relation of nicotine yield of cigarettes to blood nicotine concentrations in smokers. M A Russell, M Jarvis, R Iyer, C Feyerabend, *Br Med J* 1980;280:972-976 (5 April)

[2] Self-regulation of smoking intensity. Smoke yields of the low nicotine, low-'tar' cigarettes. Mirjana V.Djordjevic, Jingrun Fan, Saul Ferguson and Dietrich Hoffmann *Carcinogenesis* vol.16 no.9 pp.2015-2021, 1995.

[3] See, for example, Chapters 7-9 in *Adaptive dynamics: The theoretical analysis of behavior.* J. E. R. Staddon, MIT Press, 2001 and Zanutto, B. S., Staddon, J. E. R. (2007) Bang-Bang Control of Feeding: Role of hypothalamic and satiety signals. *PLoS Computional Biology,* 3(5): e97.

[4] Rose Cipollone got lung cancer after a lifetime of smoking. She claimed to have been misled by big tobacco, despite the warnings on every pack. After several back and forth rulings, the case was considered a partial victory for both sides. She got some compensation, the tobacco companies got recognition that smoking was the responsibility of the smoker. Nevertheless, the case opened the door for

tobacco cases – and the complaints of "Research" and other disaffected employees – hundreds of thousands of incriminating tobacco-company documents, many supposedly sealed under attorney-client privilege but released via court order, became public knowledge. In 1994 Scruggs got hold of roughly 4000 pages of documents stolen by a paralegal between 1988 and 1992 from the Kentucky law firm working for Brown and Williamson. Edell, with the support of a sympathetic judge, exploited a much expanded discovery process that also allowed him to share industry documents with other cases. These pilfered papers were to play a devastating role in future litigation.

The schizophrenia of the tobacco companies puzzled even their opponents. "Why collect so much information [about the ill-effects of smoking]?...It couldn't do anything except get them into trouble" one plaintiff's attorney commented. As Martha Derthick puts it "[Philip Morris] wanted to know, but the legal side did not want to tell."[1] It's worth pausing to ask who are the good guys here: Philip Morris, whose scientists wanted to understand how cigarettes work, how and why they have the effects they do and perhaps use the knowledge to make a safer cigarette. Or the lawyers on both sides, who were concerned not with knowledge, but simply with defeating their opponents? I look at the implications of this impasse for real research on smoking safety in the last chapter.

---

later real victories by sick smokers. http://www.law.cornell.edu/supct/html/90-1038.ZO.html

[1] *Up in Smoke* (2002), pp. 60-61.

Chapter 6

The Tobacco Master Settlement Agreement

Anti-tobacco litigation has happened in three phases. The first phase was the hundreds of individual tort cases brought against the tobacco companies from the mid-1950s through late 1992, prompted by a scientific consensus confirming smoking as a certain cause of lung cancer and probable contributor to a variety of lesser ailments. Pathetic individuals, stricken with cancer or emphysema, often breathing through laryngeal tubes, seeking compensation for their condition, were wheeled before juries that for a while were uniformly unsympathetic. The tobacco companies won every case, even the *Cipollone* landmark (although there were ambiguities enough in the final ruling to open the door to later litigation). This run continued after Federal Trade Commission (FTC)-enforced warning labels appeared on every cigarette pack in 1965. These warnings bolstered the so-called "preemption defense," so that every jury blamed the (supposedly informed) smoker, not the manufacturer of the sickness-inducing product.

But as the bad press for 'big tobacco' mounted, juries – and, more importantly, judges – became more and more sympathetic to sick smokers, which paved the way for the second phase, the *class-action* suit. Aggregating cases into a class was attractive to plaintiffs' lawyers for three reasons. First, the best evidence for the cancer-causing effect of smoking is statistical – although even with good statistical evidence, juries may act irrationally. But irrational bias in favor of sick plaintiffs was a plus for their attorneys in tobacco cases. In the case of supposedly cancer-causing breast implants, for example, juries often found for plaintiffs even though available evidence showed that the presence of silicone breast implants was statistically unrelated to the incidence of breast cancer[1]. I recall hear-

---

[1] "Silicone Breast Implants Are Not Linked to Breast Cancer Risk" http://www.cancer.gov/newscenter/pressreleases/2000/siliconebreast

ing a post-trial TV interview that went something like this: Question to juror: "Did you understand that breast cancer is as common among women who did not have implants as women who did?" Juror: "Yes." Question: "So why did you find for the plaintiff?" Juror: "Well, she was so sick!" In other words, the sickness of the plaintiff will often bias a jury towards her, no matter who is responsible for her plight – or even if no one is responsible, as in these breast-cancer cases[1].

The suffering of smoking 'victims' outweighed all other considerations for many juries. As I pointed out earlier, identifying smoking as the cause of any particular plaintiff's ailment is almost impossible. Absent a proven causal link, plaintiffs must rely entirely on the sympathy of the jury. In a class action suit, sympathy is not even necessary, because most people are persuaded by the statistics: the much greater statistical risk of lung cancer for smokers vs. non-smokers.

Second, the mounting public sentiment that smoking is addictive weakened the assumption-of-risk defense.

And finally, the money. Lawyers like Scruggs, Motley and Edell had accumulated both experience and cash through successful class-action asbestos cases. They were looking for more lucrative targets than could be provided by individual cases and they had the money to combat the supposedly limitless resources of the tobacco companies.

Beginning with *Castano*[2] in 1994, several attempts to get a case against the tobacco companies certified as a class action failed. The first break in the dam was a different kind of case brought by Mississippi attorney general Michael Moore in May, 1994. Aided by asbestos-enriched Dickie Scruggs[3] and nine other law firms, all working on a contingency-

---

[1] This is an almost instinctive reaction to a painful stimulus. Many studies have shown that a pair of lab rats in a cage, given a brief electric shock to their feet, will immediately attack one another. (Ulrich, R. E. and Azrin, N. H. Reflexive fighting in response to aversive stimulation. *J. exp. Anal. Behav.*, 1962, 5, 511-520.) Both rats and people will immediately blame something bad on the most obvious cause. But people, unlike rats, are able to step back and weigh the evidence – if they so choose.

[2] http://tobaccodocuments.org/profiles/litigation/castano.html

[3] Mr. Scruggs, whose brother-in-law is onetime Republican Mississippi senator Trent Lott, may have owed his great success to more than raw legal talent. In 2008 and 2009 he pled guilty to two judicial bribery charges. He is currently serving seven years in prison.

fee basis – plus Professor Laurence Tribe of the Harvard Law School, working pro bono – Moore brought a class action suit against the American Tobacco company and others. Moore's incentive structure, his payoff matrix[1], was of course highly skewed. Because most of his legal help was free, the cost to his office and the state of Mississippi was negligible, but the potential payoff was hundreds of millions of dollars in compensatory and punitive damages. It was a no-brainer.

Moore's suit claimed that the tobacco companies had been "unjustly enriched" by selling cigarettes, because their product caused smokers to incur medical costs that were paid in part by the state. Like environmental pollution, smoking-induced disease is what economists term an *externality*. Hence, Moore argued, the tobacco companies, just like coal-fired power companies, are liable. Some portion of their profits is therefore unjust and should be returned to the people (less legal expenses, of course).

The huge payoffs promised by Moore's legal innovation, and the continued willingness of armies of well-funded tort lawyers to help for free, soon prompted other state attorneys general to follow Mississippi's example. This third phase of collective action, after several legislative twists and turns, ended in a failure of the US Congress to pass controlling legislation (the McCain bill). This should have ended the matter, since interstate compacts are supposed to be approved by Congress. But no matter, the issue was finally resolved by the inter-state tobacco Master Settlement Agreement of 1998[2].

Why did the tobacco companies agree to pay prodigious sums of money? Would they, as they feared, begin to lose future product-liability cases? What form did the settlement take? Let's see.

The MSA regulated tobacco on a national scale with no legislative input whatever. It was a voluntary agreement between present – and future (though they were not consulted!) – tobacco companies to accept a wide set of restrictions and pay large sums of money into funds distributed to the participating states. The payments are sales-dependent: the more ciga-

---

[1] 'Payoff matrix' is a common technical term referring to the rewards and punishments associated with the two choices and two outcomes facing a decision-maker: act vs. don't act, and the corresponding outcomes — making up a 4-cell matrix.

[2] http://en.wikipedia.org/wiki/Tobacco_Master_Settlement_Agreement

rettes they sell, the more the producers must pay. Forty six states joined the original agreement; the remaining four had separate but similar agreements. Some of the funds were supposed to serve health-related purposes, such as anti-smoking education, but the rules were written so broadly that the revenues could be, and are, used for almost anything. North Carolina, for example, used half the money for something called the Golden LEAF Foundation[1], whose "mission is to promote the social welfare of North Carolina's citizens and to receive and distribute funds for economic impact assistance to economically affected or tobacco-dependent regions of North Carolina" – basically a slush fund. An early project supported by Golden LEAF is on wine-making at Surry College; more recently it has supported efforts to bring high-speed broadband to rural areas. Worthy purposes, no doubt, but not exactly health-related.

Another part of the MSA was allocated to reward those states who had been most aggressive in their prosecutions. A third part comprised annual payments through 2025. The total sum of money involved was prodigious, on the order of 240 *billion* dollars of which the contingency-fee lawyers got between $13 and $70 billion according to different accounts.

The MSA appears to violate both Article 1, Section 10 of the constitution barring compacts between states[2] as well as federal anti-trust statutes (it enforces a legal cartel[3]); and the financial burdens it imposes are borne by individuals not party to the agreement, namely smokers: "Tobacco companies have purchased, with smokers' money, permission to raise prices collusively and suppress competition."[4] The tobacco companies agreed to give up numerous constitutional rights: not to advertise or oth-

---

[1] http://www.goldenleaf.org/ There have been several recent criticisms of the Golden Leaf, e.g.,
http://www.wsicweb.com/index.php?option=com_content&view=article&id=430:golden-lecronyism-and-corruption-revealed-&catid=1:latest&Itemid=2

[2] It is not, of course a literal compact between the states, only between the states' attorneys general. But it is indistinguishable from one in its actual effects – restraining trade, compensatory payments, etc.

[3] Not that government-mandated cartels are a rarity: think Taxi Medallions in New York and similar restrictions in most other cities.

[4] Constitutional and antitrust violations of the multistate tobacco settlement. Thomas C. O'Brien, Cato Institute *Policy Analysis,* 371, May 18, 2000. See also Puff, the Magic Settlement: The joy of enormous tobacco fees. Walter Olson, *Reason*, January 2000.

erwise promote their product, not to oppose possible future legislation restricting their product, not to lobby – in short, not to object to the terms of the agreement or aid in any legal efforts to undo it.

Not that they had much reason to object, in fact. The MSA document[1] is a manipulative *meisterwerk*: 285 pages of legalese that conceals much of its meaning from all but the most masochistically tenacious inquirer. But the guts of the deal are clear: it is in essence a protection racket (extortion). You (the tobacco companies) pay me (the states and trial lawyers) a large amount of money. In return you get protection from competitors (the agreement forms a cartel) and from state lawsuits. The beauty of it all is that the targets of the extortion, the tobacco companies, did not have to pay the cost themselves.

The major companies were free – no, not free, *required* – to pay the piper by squeezing the smoker, without fear of competition from pesky newcomers not party to the agreement. Possibly cigarette sales would fall slightly as prices rose. But, demand for cigarettes being rather inelastic[2], profits need not fall at all. Indeed, given the freedom to raise prices afforded by a cartel, they might even increase! Thus the tobacco companies had neither the means nor the motive to object to the agreement.

It is obvious why the states' attorneys general, the recipients of generous protection money, would be happy to give up the right to further suits against big tobacco. It is only slightly less obvious why the tobacco companies would agree to pay up, rather than risking hundreds of lawsuits. It is not obvious at all why fresh new companies, untainted by the charges leveled against the old and not liable for the torts of which they had been found guilty, could not now spring up to challenge them. The MSA took care of that.

The tobacco companies caved because of fear and greed. The revelations of duplicity in the thousands of pages of leaked and stolen documents, the massive contradiction between their public and private statements, such as their witless efforts to conceal the bad effects of smoking, the damning scientific facts on cigarettes' harmful effects on smokers, and

[1] E.g., http://ag.ca.gov/tobacco/msa.php

[2] I.e., *x*% rise in price produces less than *x*% drop in sales. In fact sales did not drop significantly following the MSA.

even non-smokers[1], and the then-accepted fact that smoking is addictive and smokers thus robbed of free will – all this had produced in the public mind just the image that the FDA's Kessler had hoped to create: big tobacco as greedy, lying and heartless purveyors of death to a hapless, helpless and innocent public.

Without the MSA, the companies faced an uncertain future. An unknown number of class action suits from the states, tried in the states' own courts. Hundreds of individual suits were ongoing. If the companies could be held harmless from state suits and protected from competition, if their image could be somewhat refurbished – and without losing, indeed perhaps even making, money ... to the companies the choice must have seemed obvious.

But what about those pesky newcomers? In a nice summary of the problem and the solution, *Fortune's* Roger Parloff[2] writes:

> If the MSA imposed no corresponding obligation on [potential competitors], they would suddenly have a huge price advantage and their shares could be expected to grow explosively, reducing the states' MSA income and gradually undermining all the other goals of the MSA as well. So the challenge was to lure these other players into signing the MSA or to impose a similar financial burden on them.. The solution was a devilishly clever and maddeningly complicated array of carrot-and-stick mechanisms. The main carrot was sensible enough: Any company that signed would be assured that the MSA states could never sue it seeking Medicaid reimbursement. In addition, any wholesaler or retailer that dealt with an MSA signatory would also never have to worry about being sued by the state. In practice, this creates a powerful incentive for wholesalers and retailers to deal only with MSA signatories. (To this day [2005], nearly all major chains of convenience stores,

---

[1] Not true, but widely believed.

[2] Is the $200 Billion Tobacco Deal Going Up in Smoke? The states are addicted to the money it provides. But the comically convoluted settlement is riddled with problems, and judges' patience for it is wearing thin. Roger Parloff *Fortune Magazine*, March 7, 2005.

drugstores, discounters, and groceries refuse to handle nonparticipants' brands.)

For retailers to go along with this may be sensible, but just think for a moment about what an extraordinary provision it is. Retailer A, selling cigarettes from Liggett, say, is immune from legal action by the state, but retailer B, selling essentially an identical product from company X, which is not part of the MSA, is not. It sounds more like Tony Soprano than American justice: retailer A buys protection, paid for by the customer, and at the expense of retailer B and non-participating producers. Some less imaginative, or perhaps just more honest, states took the direct route, simply forbidding MSA non-signers from selling cigarettes in the state[1].

In addition to incentives for early signers, the agreement whacks recalcitrant newcomers. Parloff writes:

> To eliminate any price advantage for the companies that still refused to sign – the nonparticipating manufacturers – the MSA drafters added another twist: Each MSA state, as a condition of receiving its full MSA payments, would have to pass a law requiring nonparticipants to pay a per-cigarette "escrow deposit" nearly equal to the levy on participants. (Incredibly, the MSA also specifies that if any judge strikes down an escrow law as unconstitutional, that state can lose up to 65% of its MSA payments – an incentive for elected state judges to uphold those laws.)

There's much more, but you get the idea. Every detail of the MSA was tailored to protect the tobacco majors from competition and to allow them to extract from their customers the money needed for the MSA's massive payouts to the states and their contingency-fee attorneys.

As the years have passed these carefully crafted defenses have begun to erode somewhat. Small new companies have sprung up; most refused to sign on to the MSA. The MSA has been challenged in court a few times

[1] E.g., Pennsylvania: http://www.allbusiness.com/retail-trade/foodstores/4481702-1.html

since 1998, but so far unsuccessfully[1]. Although the states continue to pile up payments, their future has begun to look less secure. The Wall Street Journal reported in 2011 on the fight by one small cigarette maker against MSA-mandated fees[2]. But don't underestimate the anesthetic effect on the legal system of large sums of money for states and lawyers. Despite these challenges, the annual MSA payments increased from $7 billion to $8 billion from 2007 to 2008. It was a mere $6.4 billion in 2010, but whether this trend will continue is uncertain.

---

[1] Is the $200 Billion Tobacco Deal Going Up in Smoke? Roger Parloff *Fortune Magazine*, March 7, 2005.

[2] See, for example, *Regulation by litigation.* A. P. Morriss, B. Yandle and A. Dorchak (Eds.) Yale, U.P., 2009. p. 154. Florida Cigarette Maker Battles Proposed State Fees (*WSJ*, MARCH 15, 2011).

Chapter 7

Private Health, Public Disgrace

The Ethics of Smoking Policy

The MSA violates every kind of moral, legal and public-interest principle. The cost data on which it is based are false; many of the health claims that underpin it are either false or impossible to verify; the costs it imposes are discriminatory; and its effects on health research have been extremely destructive.

Truth: The tobacco companies won hundreds of individual product-liability cases before 1992 because juries believed smokers were responsible for their habit. The companies might well have continued to win, but their questionable behavior, the destruction of their image by Kessler and the tort lawyers, the addiction charge, and the (invalid) medical-cost argument invented by Mississippi's Attorney General Michael Moore, opened a chasm before them over which they were unwilling to leap. The resulting tobacco Master Settlement Agreement is not only based on a falsehood, but negates its own moral basis to advance health goals. The money it raises flows largely into general expenditures.

I have argued that smoking is not a public health problem; it is a private health problem. It imposes no cost on government providers of health care. Indeed, the evidence is that there is even some saving: smokers, and to a slightly lesser extent, obese people, cost *less* in health care over their lifetimes than van Baal et al.'s "healthy-living" cohort.[1] What's more, even if smokers cost *more* for their health care, the state should have no interest so long as they pay the cost themselves. Michael Moore's argument is just flat wrong. And it was known to be wrong even in 1995, al-

---

[1] Lifetime medical costs of obesity: prevention no cure for increasing health expenditure. Baal et al. (2008), op. cit.

though the evidence then was not as strong as it is now. But, amazingly, neither the plaintiffs *nor even the defendants* (the tobacco companies) – were, for the most part – interested in listening. And at least one judge refused to allow comparative-cost evidence to be introduced into court.

The basic facts are straightforward. Smokers' health care costs more at every age, but the difference is relatively small, less than 10% up to age 55 or so[1]. The big difference is lifetime cost – which is what matters. Lifetime cost is much less (as I pointed out in Chapter 4) because most health costs are incurred towards the end of life, and smokers live 6-10 years less on average than nonsmokers. When the extra taxes they pay and the government pensions they don't receive are added in, smokers in fact represent a big financial win for the non-smoking community.

Harvard legal economist Kip Viscusi presented a version of this argument in 1995. The Mississippi legal team was not happy about it. Indeed, they were outraged. In the 1995 *Memorandum* that launched their litigation effort, they wrote: "A credit to the cigarette industry for any monetary savings in elderly health care, as well as other savings resulting in the premature deaths of smokers, is utterly repugnant to a civilized society and must be rejected *on grounds of public policy*..."[2] (my italics) Denouncing Viscusi's argument as "perverse and depraved" the Mississippians stigmatized it as a request for a "early death credit."

Set aside for the moment the *chutzpah* of a bunch of private-jet lawyers rich on the backs of smokers complaining about the morality of their opponents' defense. How else should the smokers' case be made? The defense to a financial-cost argument has to be...a financial-cost argument. The Mississippi legal claim was not moral but financial, not individual but public. Although the attorney general made every effort to perfume his claim with an odor of sanctity, at bottom it was, as his own statement affirms, a matter of the state's *public financial loss* – to which the only adequate response is a counterclaim that the state had in fact made a public financial *gain*.

The plaintiffs' attorneys were outraged, but we might want to save our own outrage for the fact that the MSA continues to extract billions of dol-

---

[1] Baal et al. (2008), Figure 1.
[2] Viscusi (2002), p. 87.

lars from millions of mostly poor smokers on the basis of a false premise and a false promise of health benefits. Unfortunately, the fallacy of the plaintiffs' moral argument seems to have eluded even some of our most famous political philosophers. Perhaps because the evils of smoking have become dogma among intellectual elites, distinguished Harvard ethicist Professor Michael Sandel, whose course on Justice is viewed worldwide on the internet, evidently shares the Mississipians' outrage. In 2009 he used the 2001 Philip Morris study that showed smokers to be a profit for the Czech government (see Chapter 4) as an indictment of cost-benefit analysis in matters concerning health[1]. Sandel did not differentiate between voluntary harm, such as smoking, and the involuntary harm caused by things like pollution or toxic food. The state has an obvious interest in air and food quality; it should have none at all in what soap you use – or whether or not you smoke.

Nor did the professor seem to be aware of the distinction between public health and private health. A public-health issue is one where private action imposes a cost on the community. Cost-benefit analysis should be mandatory for making public-health policy. In the case of private health, private action has no discernible effect on the wider community. Government should leave such behavior alone. Smoking, as we have seen, is a private-health issue.

Apparently lawyers from R. J. Reynolds and Philip Morris contacted Viscusi[2] about the cost issue after reading the Mississippi diatribe, but since they ultimately settled for the MSA, the matter seems never to have been debated in court. The point was raised again in a 1998 Minnesota tobacco trial, when Judge Kenneth Fitzpatrick refused to allow comparative-cost information in court. Philip Morris's attorney (the companies were finally attentive to the economic realities) quite reasonably objected: "That's one of the most absurd rulings in these cases I've ever seen anywhere... There is absolutely no question whatsoever that cigarette smokers do not cost more in health care than nonsmokers. The net cost is less, but we're not allowed to present that evidence because we would be taking advantage of the fact that our product kills people. We're

---

[1] BBC Reith Lectures, 2009, Lecture 4.
[2] Viscusi (2002), p. 87.

not talking about taking advantage; we're talking about what the facts are."[1] But to no avail: the MSA stands, at the expense of truth.

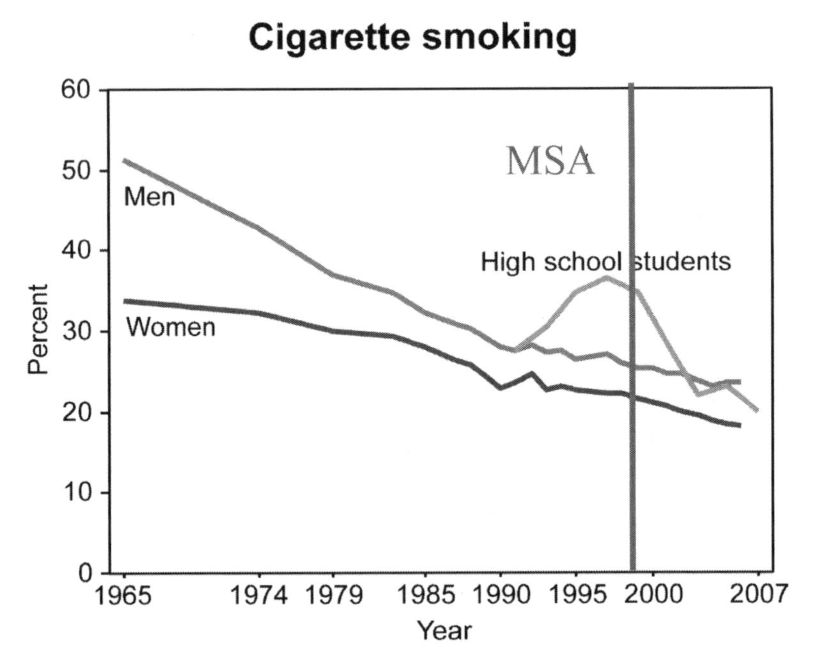

Health: The ostensible health aim of the MSA was to reduce smoking and indeed it coincided with a small decrease. From 1998 to 2004, adult smoking declined from about 27% to 23% in men and 22% to 21% in women, according to the Centers for Disease Control. But this trend began at least as far back as 1965 and continued in a more or less smooth line until 2007 (see graph above). There is no sudden drop after 1998 as might be expected if the MSA added anything to the existing anti-smoking trend. There was a steeper decline in smoking by high-schoolers – following a sharp pre-1998 increase – that did coincide with the 1998 MSA, although it began slightly earlier. But the decline just brought the high-schoolers back to the adult male level.

---

[1] Minnesota's Tobacco Trial: A Summary. By Elizabeth Stawicki. Minnesota Public Radio May 8, 1998.

It is hard to conclude that the continuing decline in adult smoking had anything whatever to do with the MSA, even though the MSA did cause an increase in the price of cigarettes. The cash thus raised from smokers was distributed equitably between the states, the lawyers, and the tobacco companies.

Of course it would have been disastrous for the agreement if there *had* been a real decrease, because a decline in smoking would have meant a decline in the revenue that nourished the whole enterprise.

Some health groups saw that the MSA was justified by a rationale that undercut itself: raising money from smokers as a way to eliminate smoking. A few health groups withdrew their support at various stages. But in the end, they were too late and the agreement went ahead.

Research: The policy aim of anti-smoking campaigners like Dr. David Kessler is in effect 'abstinence only.' They would like to see smoking cease completely. But all recognize the failure of alcohol prohibition, so no one then or now is aiming (at least openly) to criminalize smoking. Nevertheless, the abstinence-only policy has put a stop to research on making smoking safer. Indeed, the MSA forced the closure of Tobacco-Industry research groups such as the Center for Indoor Air Research, and the Council for Tobacco Research.

As we have seen, smokers, unlike many other drug users, do not engage in socially undesirable behavior – other than smoking itself, which has indeed become repugnant to many non-smokers. But smoke-aversion is a problem easily solved by adequate provision of non-smoking public spaces. Nevertheless, anti-smoking health activists have no problem with stigmatizing and being judgmental about smokers. To them, all smokers are guilty and abstinence is the only option.

The contrast between research on HIV/AIDS and research on what might be called "safe smoking" is instructive. Both smoking-induced illness and HIV are problems that are as much behavioral as biological: "The spread of HIV infection…is the product of human behaviors enacted in social contexts…The epidemic is thus as much a social and behavioral phenomenon as it is a biological one." concluded a National Academy of Science study in 1989[1]. HIV, which is not in fact very infectious, is spread

[1] *AIDS, sexual behavior and intravenous drug use*. C. F. Turner, H. G. Miller & L. E. Moses. National Academy Press, 1989.

by illegal drug use with infected needles, or by sexual promiscuity. By sexual promiscuity, I mean unprotected sex in which at least one partner has had sex with at least one other partner who has in turn had sex with another. Polygamy (multiple wives) and polyandry (multiple husbands) are OK, as well as monogamy, so long as no party has sex outside the rules. (I use the term "monogamy" for simplicity, but behavior, not legality, is what matters.) 'Straight' vs. 'gay' is irrelevant except for the fact that extreme promiscuity seems (at least before the epidemiology of AIDS became clear) to be much more common among male homosexuals than people with other sexual preferences[1]. It doesn't much matter whether the promiscuity is heterosexual or homosexual, promiscuity itself is the problem. Thus a clean-needle, polygamous, polyandrous, or monogamous, society in which pre-marital chastity and sexual fidelity are the norms will limit the spread of AIDS.

The patterns of behavior that permit the spread of AIDS were once condemned as immoral in many, if not most, human societies. Nowadays taboos like these are dismissed as prejudice. But many of them may in fact have a pre-historical evolutionary origin as public-health measures. Societies without such prohibitions may have been weakened by disease while those that enforced them flourished. In other words, some of these 'prejudices' may once have had an objective basis. Now, with advances in medicine, many feel that prohibitions against, for example, sexual promiscuity or drug use, can only be justified for religious reasons. Hence they are a continuing source of conflict.

There are two behavioral approaches to combating AIDS. One is via the technology of "safe sex" – condoms, and so forth – which is universally supported by health campaigners. For drug users, hygienic 'clean needles' are often supplied to drug users, even when drug use is itself illegal[2]. The other approach is 'just say no' programs that promote sexual abstinence. But there has been little or no support for 'just-say-no' in the US public-health community. Indeed, the stigma suffered by AIDS victims in many countries, which is presumably some deterrent to AIDS-spreading behavior, is usually deplored – because it attaches to both the

---

[1] http://www.cdc.gov/hiv/topics/surveillance/incidence.htm
[2] See, for example, the World Health Organization report: http://www.who.int/hiv/pub/prev_care/effectivenesssterileneedle.pdf

innocent and the guilty, victims who engage in AIDS-promoting behavior as well as those who do not. Stigma also supposedly deters sufferers from seeking medical help. So advocacy of 'safe sex' is the dominant policy option.

I suspect that many health professionals are unwilling to appear judgmental about sexual behavior for cultural reasons – the culture of the profession, that is. This reluctance to judge may be an example of the self-selecting survival behavior that many professions engage in, often unconsciously. For example, psychotherapists of all ideological stripes decry the use of even mild punishment with children[1], thus facilitating some children's bad behavior and increasing the need for…psychotherapists. In the AIDS case, medical professionals, by downplaying behavioral change, increase demand for medical help. Interestingly, abstinence is quite widely promoted in programs directed at third-world countries – countries that cannot, of course, afford to pay for much medical help.

Most AIDS sufferers are responsible for their own illness, in the sense that they could have avoided it by using sterile needles or condoms or avoiding promiscuous sex. But some leave behind innocent dependents, and a few sufferers, faithful wives of infected husbands, for example, who are not responsible for their infection. It is these innocent victims that make AIDS a public health problem and one, unlike smoking, that does cost society because sufferers often die while young, with young families.

I have argued that smoking is a private-health issue. To a large extent, so is AIDS. But in practice, both are considered public-health issues. Do they therefore receive the same kind and amount of research effort? By no means.

HIV/AIDS killed a relatively small number of people in the US even before advances in treatment. Smoking kills a much larger number, albeit at later ages. The federal government has spent generously on HIV/AIDS research, more than $2 billion in 2007 alone, in addition to large sums

---

[1] See for example criticism of B. F. Skinner's dismissal of punishment in *B.F. Skinner: consensus and controversy.* Edited by Sohan Modgil, Celia Modgil. Falmer Press, Taylor & Francis, 1987, e.g., Chapter 8 by Douglas Bethlehem: Scolding the Carpenter. See also Staddon, J *The New Behaviorism,* in press, and Staddon, J. (1995) On responsibility and punishment. *The Atlantic Monthly*, Feb., 88-94. A longer version is available as Staddon (1999) On Responsibility in Science and Law. http://dukespace.lib.duke.edu/dspace/handle/10161/3392

spent by such as the Gates Foundation. Huge medical advances have been made in controlling HIV, exemplified by the productive lives of famous sufferers such as writer Andrew Sullivan and sports stars Magic Johnson and Greg Louganis.

In contrast, the government has not spent a nickel looking for a "safe" cigarette. It has spent plenty documenting, and exaggerating, the dangers of smoking – with mixed results, as we saw earlier. Philip Morris did some in-house research on smoking safety until they stopped in the 1990s – for fear of seeming to acknowledge the dangers of smoking. PBS's NOVA commented in 2008:

> [T]he safe cigarette has been stymied by the very groups who are most concerned about the health effects of smoking: anti-tobacco groups and public health officials. The cigarette industry's efforts to market safer cigarettes have been met with fierce opposition by anti-tobacco activists, who want to see such products labeled as nicotine delivery devices and subjected to government regulations. Although the opposition of health groups to a safe cigarette would seem contradictory, it is borne out of a deep mistrust of the cigarette companies, whose strategy of denial over the years has created a credibility gap with the public health community.[1]

Well after it became literally incredible to deny the harmful effects of smoking, Philip Morris resumed safe-cigarette research. But, despite those '400,000 preventable deaths' each year[2], the "just say no" policy of health groups and their hostility to tobacco and the tobacco companies has stifled any move to extend NIH funding to safe-smoking research. Stigmatizing of smoking and smokers has thus had a devastating effect on public health as the public health community itself defines it.

How even-handed is government research policy? Do smoking and AIDS attract research dollars in proportion to the number of Americans they kill? No – and the disparity is shocking. The number of AIDS deaths

[1] http://www.pbs.org/wgbh/nova/cigarette/history.html

[2] The 400,000 per year smoking death toll is wildly exaggerated; nevertheless, the true figure is nevertheless much larger than the 20,000 a year or so who succumb to AIDS.

is an order of magnitude at least smaller than deaths attributed to smoking. Yet billions are spent on the former, essentially zero on the latter.

As I pointed out earlier, public policy is supposed to serve moral ends. Health policy certainly aims to save life. Few would quarrel with that. But an ethicist might also ask: What other values, what morality, are favored by existing policy? Drug use and sexual promiscuity are activities that conduce to the spread of AIDS. Are these activities promoted by government research? No one would say so, yet a cure for AIDS makes them safer. They are encouraged by current policy. What are the values on the other side, the activities of smokers, that would be encouraged by making smoking safer? The pleasure of puffing on a cigarette. US research policy implies that the first set of pleasures is hundreds of times more valuable than the second. Is that fair? Is it even sensible? Go figure.

...liberty and the pursuit of happiness: "[I]t is inconceivable that government would permit the new introduction of a product known beforehand to be as addictive and deadly as the cigarette..."[1] So wrote Professor John Slade, a public health expert, claiming that cigarettes are sold now only for historical reasons. I am relieved that Prof. Slade was[2] not also a legal expert. Where is it written in the US Constitution that it is the government's duty to protect a responsible individual from something whose dangers are known, does no harm to others and gives pleasure to himself? But this is undoubtedly the prevailing view in the public-health community: that government should infantilize the American people by preventing them from having access to *any* product that is known to pose a risk, whether the risk is private or public. Anathema especially attaches to anything related to smoking. The latest variation on this theme is the chorus of health-group protests against e-cigarettes – electrical nicotine-delivery devices less unpleasant to others and possibly less dangerous to

---

[1] John Slade, Marketing policies. In *Regulating tobacco* (2001) p. 76. He's not the only one. In the May 23, 2012, *Financial Times,* John Tyndall wrote: "Let us imagine that tobacco was discovered today and entrepreneurs endeavoured to manufacture and distribute cigarettes. Would they be allowed? Would it be legal? I suggest that anyone involved in the above endeavour would be put in the same category as heroin dealers." Yes, that is a problem...

[2] Anti-smoking campaigner and non-smoker Professor John Slade died prematurely of a stroke at the age of 52 in 2002.

the smoker than tobacco cigarettes.[1] The innocent pleasure that smokers get from their risky habit weighs not at all with these folk.

Deception: One of the most damning charges against 'big tobacco' was its attempt to conceal from the public the addictive and illness-causing properties of cigarettes. This accusation raises not one question, but three: Did big tobacco in fact conceal any more than was the custom among other advertisers at the time? What other information was available to the public? And, finally, what *blame* should attach to the tobacco companies?

Undoubtedly from the 1950s, when the carcinogenic effects of cigarettes became well-known, through the early 1960s, the tobacco companies did make strenuous efforts to conceal, or at least to downplay, the illness-causing properties of cigarettes. However, truth-in-advertising during that period was not enforced nearly as vigorously by the Federal Trade Commission as it was later, so it's by no means clear that the cigarette companies were any worse in this respect than many others. Nor is it clear that they were all lying. Many tobacco executives in the 1950s and 1960s, along with pre-eminent statistician R. A. Fisher (quoted in Chapter 2), genuinely believed that cigarettes were harmless. But post-1965, increasingly stark, not to say exaggerated, warnings were mandated to appear on every cigarette packet. Tobacco ads were increasingly limited as to content and location. TV cigarette ads were banned and other ads could no longer say anything about health. Promoting health aspects of cigarettes was therefore limited to marketing innovations like filter tips and 'lite' labels after 1970 or so.

What did the public actually know during that period? Based on survey data, Viscusi has argued at length that post-1970, if not before, the public was perfectly well aware of the dangers of smoking. Cigarettes were not called coffin nails and cancer sticks for nothing. Nevertheless, some disagree. In 2000 Viscusi's analysis was severely criticized by Paul Slovic, a distinguished decision theorist. In response, Viscusi concluded "as is clear from the life expectancy loss statistics reported in Slovic's [data], both smokers and the sample overall overestimate the life expectancy

[1] Controversy Swirls Around E-Cigarettes . *WSJ*, June 2, 2009.

loss associated with smoking."[1] To which Slovic responded by pointing out that people show 'optimism bias': they think they are personally less at risk than the statistics indicate, that they are more likely to quit smoking in the future than they really are, and don't understand that it gets harder to quit the more you smoke. So, smokers know, even exaggerate, the stats but think they're immune anyway.

What are we to make of this clash of experts? Undoubtedly most people do not fully comprehend statistics of almost any kind. Many studies have shown that people are at least as unclear, and optimistic, about their driving skills, likely future value of their houses, probable duration of their marriages, future economic prospects – and future health – as they are about their future as cigarette smokers. So in what sense does smokers' failure to grasp the full meaning of available statistics implicate the tobacco companies? Why are tobacco companies to blame for misleading them when people often appear to mislead themselves? It all depends, I suppose, on whether we expect the companies to just present accurate information in an accessible form or whether, in addition, we hold them responsible for consumers' scores on some kind of smoking-and-health quiz. In other words, where does the responsibility of the vendor end and that of the consumer begin?

Traditionally, the obligation of the honest vendor has been to tell the truth and make sure that all buyers get to see it. The responsibility of the vendor is to inform, of the buyer to understand. To go beyond this, to hold the vendor responsible not just for providing information but for the buyer's actual state of knowledge, treats the buyer as not responsible and imposes an excessive – and mostly unnecessary – burden on commerce in general. And consumers would surely find it annoying to be tested on their comprehension of safety instructions.

The deception case against the tobacco companies is at best equivocal. But there is of course, unequivocal evidence of deception and concealment on the other side. Tobacco-related internet sites accessed from the UK used to require 'older-than-18' certification before you can see them.

---

[1] Comment: The perils of qualitative smoking risk measures. W. Kip Viscusi, *Journal of Behavioral Decision Making,* Vol, 13, 267-271 (2000). Rejoinder: the perils of Viscusi's analyses of smoking risk perceptions. Paul Slovic, *J. Behav. Dec. Making*, 13: 273-276 (2000).

Alcohol-related sites have no such restriction, however. Some tobacco-related sites are not accessible at all in the UK. Swiss cigar-maker Davidoff used to come up with "Welcome to davidoff.com We are sorry due to national legal restrictions we can not grant you access to our Website www.davidoff.com. Thank you for your understanding." Now they just ask you for your age – so at least honest young people are protected!

Movie-poster pictures of fashion icon Coco Chanel, a lifelong (1883-1971) smoker, were recently doctored to remove her cigarette: "France has a law against depicting smoking in advertising – so to avoid prosecution, the company that sells ads on Parisian public transportation banned a poster featuring Audrey Tautou as Coco Chanel holding a cigarette." [1] In Paris the poster was replaced with a "more anodyne" one with no cigarette; in the UK, the cigarette was photoshopped into a pen. French comedic actor Jacques Tati's pipe suffered a similar fate a few years ago. These are only the most recent of many Orwellian attempts to erase smoking from history. They have been strikingly unsuccessful. But they do attest to the dishonesty of smoking opponents.

Democracy and Justice: The great scandal of the MSA is that the people who have to pay its huge costs – smokers – had no say at all in the agreement. The MSA is "tyranny of the majority" and "taxation without representation" on a scale that dwarfs the colonial imposts that prompted the Boston tea party. It's hard to see any moral justification for this aspect of the MSA that does not remove smokers from the ranks of responsible citizens. "It's for your own good" did not exculpate Torquemada and the Spanish Inquisition. As Jacob Sullum eloquently pointed out when the disgraceful tobacco MSA first came about, good intentions do not excuse anti-smoking, and anti-smoker, zealots[2]. "It's for your own good" treats smokers like children or the mentally ill. I doubt that Winston Churchill, Dwight Eisenhower and Ayn Rand would have been altogether happy to be thus categorized. In fact, the MSA did nothing for smokers, even failing to reduce their numbers below historical trends. At least Torquemada guaranteed salvation to sincere converts. (And who is to say they did not receive it?)

---

[1] http://jezebel.com/5223447/coco-avant-chanel-poster-banned-in-paris.

[2] *For your own good: The anti-smoking crusade and the tyranny of public health.* By Jacob Sullum, The Free Press, 1998.

Incentives: The MSA came about because it presented a no-lose proposition to Michael Moore and the other states' attorneys general. They risked no real cost if their suits lost. Skewed incentives – what I have called the malign hand, in contrast to Adam Smith's invisible hand – are very dangerous indeed. Incentives should be the very first thing law-givers look at before they pass legislation. Of course, the often-skewed incentives to which they themselves respond may also be a problem – one for which there is no easy solution.

Emotion: **Smokers are the new Niggers:** During the confirmation hearings for Supreme Court Justice nominee Sonia Sotomayor in 2009 there was much public discussion of the role of "empathy" and "emotion" as helpful ingredients in judicial judgments. Well, emotion certainly did play a large role in the MSA. Unfortunately it took the form of an almost pathological hatred for the tobacco companies – by litigators, by health activists and eventually by much of the public at large. Compassion, even respect, for smokers has also been notably absent. Smokers seem to be the only group against whom discrimination now is not only permitted but encouraged. Paradoxically, smokers are condemned even by those who believe they are not responsible for their addiction.

The resemblance between racial discrimination and discrimination against smokers is surprisingly close. The same factors – prejudice, money and flawed science – are involved in both. Racial prejudice began with some Europeans' distaste for dusky illiterates from distant lands. It was reinforced by first by money – the need for black slaves to make farming tobacco and cotton in the Americas a viable business. The inferior status of blacks was then further justified by bad science, "proving" their genetic inferiority. I have just traced the parallel history of prejudice against smokers. The same three factors seem to operate, albeit in a different order. First, distaste – King James' feeling that smoking is a "lothsome custome." Next came weak science, implicating smoking in every known ailment and claiming lethality for secondhand smoke. And finally *money*, the huge revenue to be raised "for their own good" from smokers.

It seems that human beings need to despise somebody. Since blacks and homosexuals are no longer available, the forces of prejudice, money and pseudoscience that victimized them can be turned on smokers (and, increasingly, the obese).

A belief they are doing God's (= public health's) work allowed many health professionals to set aside every other value in their quest to abolish smoking. The FDA's Kessler, Captain Ahab to the tobacco industry's white whale, persisted in his attempts to get control of tobacco regulation, even when it should have been obvious that the responsibility belonged to Congress, not to him. (Congress finally took it up again in 2009: by congressional mandate, the FDA now regulates tobacco.) It was this demonizing of a minority – smokers as well as 'big tobacco' – that allowed the MSA to get by with violating numerous principles of truth, fairness and the founding principles of the United States.

Postscript

This book is about the difference between public and private health. Not all health problems are public health problems. Smoking is the most striking example of a private health problem. It's risky for the smoker, but not for the rest of us. I discussed the consequences of this mis-categorization, and of the grotesquely skewed incentives created by the class-action legal process, in earlier chapters. They provide many examples of the malign hand: private good (cash for the litigants) means public bad (stigmatization and unfair taxation of smokers). This chapter summarized the ethical violations to which all this has led. Activist groups, inside as well as outside a supposedly neutral federal government, have been able to demonize both an industry and, eventually, a class of citizens. They have led us to trash truth, fairness, individual freedom, and the idea of personal responsibility. Tort lawyers and states' attorneys general achieved vast and continuing financial gains. Public health gained nothing at all. Personal freedom and scientific research lost much. In contrast to the massive effort aimed at curing HIV/AIDS, no one is now trying to understand just why cigarettes are dangerous. Safety-related smoking research is for the most part tendentious and pedestrian.

This sad history illustrates big problems in the way we deal with hot-button health-and-safety issues. The tobacco MSA was a huge malfunction of the legal and legislative systems. In response to the dangers of tobacco, supposedly authoritative public bodies, like the Surgeon General the Centers for Disease Control and the Royal College of Physicians (UK), made categorical statements that go well beyond the facts, indeed beyond any possible facts. Given its low concentration, people's intermittent exposure, the long delay before any possible bad effects – and the impossibility of controlled experiment – there is simply no way that anyone can say "there is no safe level of secondhand smoke." Yet this is now dogma. The statement "there is no safe level" is as unprovable of perfume or deodorant as of secondhand smoke. No finite number of negative experimental results can disprove it. Neither the surgeon general nor anyone else really knows, or can know. In any case, proving a negative is impossible. No number of experiments that fail to show effects on A or B can prove that some such effect on C or D could not be demonstrated by yet another experiment.

But government health authorities in this case and in many others seem incapable of admitting ignorance on a sensitive issue. When confronted with real uncertainty, they plump for the politically correct conclusion – even at the cost of truth and their own credibility.

It's worth asking, as a postscript, what would be the implications if, as the states' attorneys general contended, risky activities that exact real social costs should be paid for by those responsible? There are, after all, many risky activities, from rock climbing to sailing and motorcycling – and unprotected, promiscuous sex – that *do* incur real dollar costs to the public. Climbers and sailors must sometimes be rescued; injured or killed motorcyclists incur unnecessary medical and family-support costs; and STD sufferers must be treated, often very expensively. If we are all to be covered by universal health insurance, as seems highly likely in the US and is already the case in many other developed countries, and if smoking really were costly, a balanced tax on cigarettes (not to mention irresponsible sexual activity!) to cover the cost seems to be entirely reasonable. In the case of smoking, there should be no tax, of course, because there is in fact no social cost. But consistency demands that (for example) condom-free sex partners, motorcyclists, skiers, mountain climbers and fatties (well not fatties – their lifetime health cost is slightly below average), should also be taxed to reflect their greater health risks and social costs. Is this really a great idea?

We might also ask: is it right to force everyone to subscribe to collective health insurance[1]? Should we really deny some adventurous individuals the right to a possibly short but inexpensive life, free of insurance of any kind? Is it indeed collectively beneficial to eliminate from society, or at least to discourage, all those adventurous souls who are willing to take a risk?

And finally there is the problem of *risk* itself. Health professionals seek zero risk: no government should permit Americans to smoke, even if smokers know the risk and it affects only them. Recall Professor Slade's

[1] The problem of people who want health insurance but cannot afford it is a separate issue that requires it own remedy.

comment that if tobacco were a new drug, it would, and should, be banned. Well, this is a natural enough belief for a healer. I remember a few years ago being surprised when Dr. Marcia Angell and two health advocates objected to a proposed research study in which some African AIDS sufferers, who would otherwise have gone untreated, were to be given lower-than-standard doses of the expensive anti-HIV drug AZT to see if they would do any good. If successful, the experiment would have allowed many more AIDS victims to be helped than was then possible with the existing supply and standard doses of AZT. Yet Dr. Angell raised ethical objections to the study[1].

I should not have been surprised. Dr. Angell, one-time editor of the *New England Journal of Medicine* and a respected figure in US medical science, acted as a physician not a scientist when she objected to the study on the grounds that some subjects (the control group) would receive no drug treatment at all, receiving a placebo instead. For the physician, *any* failure to treat is wrong, irrespective of overall cost-benefit For example, not knowing which pill is best, a good clinician might well recommend several to a very sick patient, even though by doing so he could have no idea which one was effective in a cure. Bad science, but good medicine.

But policymakers should follow a different logic. The moral issue for them is whether any individual volunteer in the study would be worse off if the study were done than if it were not done. The answer for the African study is that none would have been worse off, and some might be better off. In other words, the expected cost was zero, with some expected bene-

---

[1] Angell M. The ethics of clinical research in the Third World. *N Engl J Med.* 1997;337: 847-849. Marcia Angell, *Tuskegee Revisited, WSJ,* 10/28/97. See also It's AIDS, not Tuskegee By David D. Ho, M.D. *TIME*, Monday, Sep. 29, 1997: http://www.time.com/time/magazine/article/0,9171,987069,00.html A legitimate objection to the study is that the same amount of medicine could have been applied, in full dose, to a much smaller number of sufferers. The individuals who might have been in this small group did therefore lose by the study. On the other hand, some individuals in the study who were to receive smaller-than-standard doses of the drug might benefit. And of course if the smaller dose becomes the new standard very many will benefit in the future – many more than those who might have been treated now with the standard dose. Balancing the certain cost to this small number against the benefit to the larger number possibly treatable with a below-standard dose might still lead one to reject the study. But Dr. Angell's only concern was patients in the (untreated) control group. She was apparently not willing to balance cost and benefit as a good policy maker should.

fit. Economists call this a *Pareto improvement*[1] – a no-lose proposition. The research was both ethical and in the public interest.

The views of physicians, acting as physicians rather than scientists or policymakers, in public-health policy should never be decisive, because they chant a one-note mantra of health über alles. They will often be in conflict with both good science and wise public policy. This is a lesson that the FDA's Kessler, like many other medically-trained policymakers, seems unwilling to learn. I hope this book has persuaded you that there is another and better way to look at health-related issues like smoking. If we follow it, the result will be better for society and for smokers.

---

[1] After Vilfredo Pareto (1848-1923), Italian economist and philosopher who made many important advances in mathematical and empirical economics.

WILL EUROPE
EVER FIT TOGETHER

Acknowledgements

I thank the University of York, UK, the York Public Library, Rochelle Schwartz-Bloom, Dan Cerutti, Michael Davis, Martha Derthick, Robert Glass, Peter Killeen, Ed Levin, Terrie Moffitt, Bob MacPhail, Chuck Pelon, Philip Quinlan, James Rothman, Jed Rose, Amanda Sowden, Jessica Staddon, Nick Staddon, Brian Taylor and Edward Tiryakian. Alan Baddeley made me rethink some of my arguments and Ralph Heinz has helped with creative discussions over many years and expert help on many medical issues. I thank David Boaz (and an anonymous CATO economist) for very helpful comments on the MS. I am grateful to NSF and NIH, and especially to Duke University, for research support over many years.

About the Author

John Staddon is James B. Duke Professor of Psychology, and Professor of Biology and Neurobiology, Emeritus, at Duke University. He is a Faculty Affiliate at the John Locke Foundation and Honorary Visiting Professor at the University of York (UK). He got his undergraduate degree from University College, London and his PhD in Experimental Psychology from Harvard. He has worked in many universities around the world: MIT, University of Toronto, Oxford University (UK), University of São Paulo at Riberão Preto (Brazil), the University of Mexico, the Ruhr Universität and Universität Konstanz, (Germany), and the University of Western Australia. He is a fellow of several scientific organizations, has edited two research journals and been associate or sub-editor on several others, and has received various honors. His experimental laboratory has studied interval timing in animals and people, choice behavior, the acoustics of bird song, and simulated detection of landmines. He has done theoretical work on operant and reflex conditioning, behavioral ecology, behavioral economics, memory, timing and psychobiological aspects of legal and ethical philosophy. He has written and lectured on public-policy issues such as evolution and education, IQ, traffic control, smoking and the effects of social and biological processes in finance and economics. He has published more than 200 research papers and six books, including *The Malign Hand of the Markets* (2012, McGraw-Hill), *The New Behaviorism: Mind, Mechanism and Society*. (Psychology Press, 2001, new edition forthcoming) and *Adaptive Dynamics: The Theoretical Analysis of Behavior,* (MIT/Bradford, 2001), *Adaptive Behavior and Learning* (Cambridge University Press, 1983, new edition 2010:
http://dukespace.lib.duke.edu/dspace/handle/10161/2878) and *Handbook of Operant Behavior* (with W. K. Honig), Prentice-Hall, 1977.

Website: http://fds.duke.edu/db/aas/pn/faculty/staddon